Dating for Men

Unlocking the Secrets to Meeting People in Real-Life and Using Online Dating Apps – Along with How to Attract Women on Dates by Displaying Alpha Male Confidence and Body Language

Contents

Introduction

Although this is a dating-for-men guidebook, above that, the main purpose of the book is to help you become a confident, self-assured, alpha male, a man of vision and purpose in all areas of your life, because only by being such a man can you attract women and master your dating and relationship life.

You are reading this guide because:

• You would like to know how to be confident when approaching and talking to women and you are looking for practical, actionable advice that will help you to do this with a degree of ease.

• You know the importance of self-confidence in dating and in all areas of your life but unfortunately, perhaps because of various insecurities and negative beliefs, you do not feel confident, manly, or capable of tapping into and using your masculinity to attract women or enhance your dating life.

• You have had some bad luck with women in the past—maybe a rejection or a bad breakup—and are now looking to get it right by adopting smart strategies that help you attract smart women who you connect with and that you find interesting.

- You like and want to date beautiful and interesting women but the women you want seem interested in other men, men who appear sure of what they want and know how to talk to women, a character trait you feel you lack.

- You want to know how to start online and in-person conversations with women in a manner that helps you foster a connection that goes beyond physical attraction, so that you can go out on dates with interesting women.

- You want to know what women want from men, so that you can use this knowledge to meet women online and offline and find interesting and smart women you can date and develop a relationship with—irrespective of whether your intention is to date, find love, or build a long-term relationship.

If you are reading this book in order to master any of the above areas of your dating and relationship life, you are reading the right book at the right time; but consider this:

The result you want to achieve is: *success in your dating and relationship life.* Unfortunately, because you are not self-assured or confident in your ability to meet, attract, and date fine-looking women, you have not had much success in this area of your life yet. You are now feeling frustrated and ready to give up, because the dating advice you have received thus far does not seem to be working for you.

Despite your frustrations, you are not prone to giving up on something you want badly, which is why you are reading this guide: hoping to learn actionable strategies that can help you master your dating and relationship life.

Your desire to improve and become a better man in all areas of your life is commendable and worthy of applause, because this is not something most men do. The fact that you are doing it proves you are determined and that you can achieve anything you put your mind to—if you have the right approach.

A large portion of this guidebook shall revolve around showing you how to adopt the right approach or mindset to dating and how to become an attractive man so that when you do start dating, you attract valuable women and achieve immense success in your dating and relationship life.

You see, meeting, attracting, dating, and starting long-term relationships with amazing, intelligent, drop-dead gorgeous women does not have to be difficult. In fact, dating is easier than you think because to master it, all you need to do is cultivate self-confidence by working on yourself *before* you welcome a woman into your life. We call this doing the hard work first: by dating yourself before you start dating someone else.

Dating yourself first is super important because it helps you embrace your authentic self and become someone who knows he is enough. As you can guess, once you know you are enough and that you can be happy and content without having a woman by your side, you stop wanting to date women because you are seeking external fulfilment, and start doing it because you want to share yourself and your great life with an equally great woman. When you do this, your sense of confidence improves.

This is fundamentally life changing because one of the things Gregg Michaelsen—a relationship expert, life coach, and bestselling author—notes is that confidence is the most important element in dating, and if you want to have a great dating and relationship life, you need to cultivate it before you decide to share yourself or your life with another person.

Because confidence is the secret to dating and having it changes the dating game for you, large sections of this guidebook will revolve around helping you to become a confident man. In fact, most of what we shall discuss in this guide shall in one way or another tie back to showing you how to use various strategies to become a strong confident man, a purposeful alpha male, and the kind of man that women want to meet and approach with dating in mind.

In addition to a ton of other important dating for men topics and strategies, here is a small sampling of what you shall learn from this guidebook:

• How to become a confident man and how to display this confidence using body language and mannerisms in all areas of your life; and more importantly, how to unleash and tap into the confident power within you and use it to attract women and meet new people.

• What it means to be an alpha male, why it is important, how alpha males behave and conduct themselves, and the various strategies you can employ to start polishing the alpha male within you—irrespective of your current preoccupation, looks, or life condition.

• How to get past the "I suck at dating" and the "nice guy" mentalities and instead adopt a healthy mentality that allows you to accept the fact that failing in the past does not mean your dating life shall suck forever or that rejection means you will never find a mate or love.

• How to go from a person who lacks confidence and is unsure of what to say to women to someone who can start online and offline conversations with all sorts of women, and then confidently lead these conversations toward a specific end, such as dating or a long-term relationship. This alone will help you learn how to talk to women in person and online, the signals to look out for, mistakes to avoid, and everything else you need to know in order to master the art of starting and maintaining interesting conversations with women.

• The online and offline dating mistakes you are probably making—as well as how to avoid them.

And so much more!

About This Book

This guide has three sections with various chapters within each section.

The first section, which is the most important section of this entire guidebook, covers the confidence part of the equation; it shall help you understand important dating elements like:

> • Why confidence is the secret to dating for men, what confidence means, and how to become a confident man.

> • What being an alpha male means, why it is important, and how to unleash the alpha male within you.

> • The art of body language, why it matters, how to use positive body language to attract women long before you say anything, as well as a ton of other amazing stuff that will help you become the kind of man women want to date and fall in love with.

> • How to do the hard work first by working on your insecurities and on yourself, so that you can approach women positively and with great confidence.

NOTE: Try not to skip the first section. If you do, you shall miss a lot and fail to learn about or adopt the "confident man" mindset that guarantees success in your dating and relationship life.

The second section of the guide covers the fundamentals of dating in the modern world. From this section, you will learn important elements such as:

> • Where to meet women in real-life and more importantly, how to go about approaching these women in a manner that gets you results; including how to start in-person conversations with beautiful women whether in the street, the gym, supermarket, et cetera.

> • How to use online dating apps and platforms correctly in order to get the best results. We shall discuss issues such as how to create and optimize your online dating profile, so that it stands out and is memorable, and the ins and outs of online dating, how to ask intelligent and interesting questions— including which questions to ask—and so much more.

> • The common dating mistakes that turn-off women: here we shall discuss how to get around the various dating pitfalls that men make, and what to do instead.

...And so much more!

After reading the second section of the guide and integrating it with the actionable knowledge and new mindset from the first section of the guide, the third section teaches you how to date like a pro! You will feel capable of attracting, approaching, talking to, dating and courting women from all walks of life.

Now that you know how this book will help you and the various things we intend to cover as you read along and implement what you learn, before we move on, take a moment to conduct the following exercise:

Before we start, a simple exercise.

One of the fundamental things we know and understand about the human spirit is that when we feel connected to something, when our reason(s) for wanting to achieve something is strong and bone deep, we are willing to find a way to get what we want. The same applies to your dating and relationship life.

To enhance this aspect of your life, you need to have a strong "why," a reason (or several of them) for wanting to improve your dating and relationship life.

Whether your reasons for embarking on this journey are to find love, to date, to form a long-term relationship with an amazing woman, to get back into the dating scene after being out for a long time, or to get back on the saddle after a bad breakup, do the following:

Take this moment to think about the result you want, which in this case is success in your dating and relationship life, and visualize how you will feel once you start being confident, purposeful, and capable of meeting, attracting, and dating beautiful women.

Clearly visualize how your world will change once you become an alpha male and how women respond to you positively. Let this picture saturate your mind until it comes to life. Live it, breathe it, be it: clearly visualize the successful man you want to become and then steadfastly hold on to this image.

The truth is that even if you are the most unconfident, shy, "nice guy" in existence, you can become the man you just envisioned. Yes, you can become a man who is capable of meeting women online and in real life; you can become a confident man, the kind of man that attracts and goes on as many dates as he wants with beautiful, interesting women. All you need to do is implement the various lessons and strategies you will learn from this guidebook.

Now that you are feeling pumped and sure that you have what it takes to meet, attract, approach, talk to, and date beautiful women, let us move on, so that you can start equipping yourself with the skills you need to master this area of your life.

Section 1:

Introduction to Dating for the Modern Man

If you wish to live a rich and full life; a life permeated by the actualization of your full potential and the fulfilment of all your aims as a man; a life where you build amazing relationships and date beautiful women; a life of purpose where you are a self-confident and self-assured man, listen up:

Dating isn' t complicated, we just make it so.

Although dating in the modern age seems complicated to most men, it really is not. Dating is incredibly easy—it always has been. In fact, to master your dating and relationship life, all you need to remember is the following:

To master your dating and relationship life, you need to learn how to embrace and unleash your authentic self so that you can become a confident man, an alpha male, a purposeful and driven man who is always in his element and is therefore the kind of man women want to date, love, and be with in a committed relationship.

That is it, really! If you embody this advice, you will have no trouble attracting beautiful women or creating meaningful, interesting relationships. To have a great dating and relationship life by becoming a man who can meet new people, attract and date gorgeous women, and sustain relationships, the *only* thing you need to do is learn how to *unleash your authentic self* and be a *confident man.* You need to learn how to be a confident man who feels good about himself, who knows what he wants and why he wants it!

As long as you can display a sense of self-assuredness and embody the "alpha male" or "leader" mentality—a mentality that comes from knowing yourself, trusting yourself, being sure of what you want, and believing you are enough—you will create great relationships and attract beautiful, interesting women that like you and who are ready for dating or relationships.

Once you master how to communicate your needs with respect and self-assuredness and lead with confidence, (irrespective of whether you are looking to get into a new relationship or sustain a long-term one) you should experience great success and adventure in your dating and relationship life; you should be able to attract women to you without trying too hard.

An insight into why confidence is the secret to dating.

Developing a "confident man" attitude, what we also refer to as: "becoming an alpha male of your life" or "tapping into your masculine energy or strength," can also help you in other important areas of your life, such as your career, business life, and friendships. Having a confident attitude is the quickest way to a life of fulfilled potential as a man; a life well lived and enjoyed.

Being self-confident, assured of your worth as a man, and committed to personal betterment is the secret to dating and successful relationships. This is because if you create a strong sense of self-belief—something that comes only from working on yourself—you will be a step closer to the life you have always wanted. If you master self-confidence and self-belief, you will be a step closer to a life of purpose; one where because you are purposeful and confident, you attract and date beautiful women, have happy relationships, and above all else, you live a life rich in personal fulfilment.

To become a self-confident and self-assured man, a man who can attract, engage, and excite (not trick) any woman into a date and then into a mutually beneficial relationship, you need to let go of everything you think you know about modern dating for men. Instead, you need to adopt a new approach, the kind discussed in this guide.

Here is why:

The problem with modern dating advice.

The problem with modern dating advice for men is that it focuses on teaching men how to be compliant with women, to be "nice guys," men who lack confidence and because they do not feel so good about themselves, need to date and bed a lot of women in order to feel good. Otherwise, it focuses not on teaching men how to become winners in their lives, by being purposeful and great men who can attract amazing women, but on how to "pick up" and "trick" women into bed.

That is not how dating should be and if you adopt a similar approach, it will only be a matter of time before your dating and relationship life implodes, spirals out of control, and causes distress in other important areas of your life: such as your finances, your self-esteem, your career, and your personal life. You need to change your approach.

What dating should be about.

Dating is about meeting new people not because you have an implicit need to meet women, but because you are genuinely interested in meeting new people, learning from them, and building good relationships with them.

Above all else, for the modern man, dating should be about finding who you are and doing your best to become that person. When you do this, you radiate confidence, masculinity, and self-assuredness, which makes you immensely attractive to the opposite sex.

Think of it this way: money attracts money. Likewise, strong, confident, and self-assured men attract valuable and interesting women, and if you become a strong and confident man, you will have your pick of valuable and interesting women to date.

Once you let go of the "pick up" mentality and instead adopt a mature, "confident man" approach, you shall undoubtedly experience great success in your dating and relationship life. This is because once you adopt this new mindset, you will stop trying to "trick" women into bed or relationships and shall instead strive to create mutually beneficial relationships with women who are as smart and as intelligent as you are.

You should also know that confidence with women is less about the women you approach, meet, and date, and more about you: the man you are, the man you are becoming, and the women you want to share yourself and your life with.

Confidence with women revolves around believing in yourself and in your ability to attract, talk to, and date beautiful women because you know you are a valuable man, a man who has direction in life, a man who can say "no" to things that fail to align with the life you want for yourself and "yes" to those that do.

Being confident and great at attracting, meeting, and dating beautiful women online and in person is about clearly knowing what you want, what is right for you and what is not, and willingly choosing the former over the latter. It is not about "needing women" to feel great; it is about feeling great about yourself long before you decide to meet women or to share any piece of your life with them.

The other problem with modern dating advice for men is that instead of helping men learn how to explore themselves so that they can find compatible partners; or equipping men with actionable strategies they can use to navigate the murky waters of modern dating—while still being true to their unique selves—common dating advice is often similar to this:

"After matching with a woman online, make sure the first message you send her is interesting. Make sure that the conversation you have with her is one that shows your masculinity, makes you appear confident and self-assured, and that you drive the conversation toward an actual date."

There is nothing wrong with this advice; in fact, this is great advice—but only if you come at it with a "confident man" mindset and know how to implement it in an actual scenario. Otherwise, following such advice seems too complicated; fraught with too many rules; and as you can guess, when followed improperly, such advice is likely to make you a "pick up artist" or confuse you so much that "analysis paralysis" kicks in.

Unfortunately, this advice rarely takes into account various important elements, such as:

> • What does "make your messages interesting" mean and how can you do it well when smart, modern women seem to be using confusing online dating signals? How do you make your message interesting when starting and sustaining a conversation with a total stranger is a challenge?

> • How do you determine what to say, how to say it, and when to say it in order to drive a conversation forward with a woman you are yet to meet and therefore know very little about—including what she likes and does not like and the kind of messages she is likely to respond to or overlook altogether?

> • What about instances when you are meeting women in real-life situations? What should you do to make the process easier and less confusing, and to be—or appear—masculine and confident; especially when you feel self-conscious, unconfident, and insecure of the fact that you have a failed relationship to your name?

Such advice also seems over-simplistic, lacking tangibility, and often times geared toward helping you talk to women for the sake of it—or for sex: what we call "picking up" women–instead of helping you come at the prospect from a healthy perspective, one of connecting with women you find interesting so that you can build beautiful, healthy relationships.

Confidence in dating is simple: be sure of yourself and of what you want when approaching a woman. It is not about tricking women into believing you are something you are not so that you can bed them or get into a relationship with them. Confidence in dating has never been about preying on women or using them as "emotional punching bags" that you can use to vent out your insecurities, dating frustrations, and other shortcomings. If that is your mentality, you need to drop it right now.

To achieve great success in your dating and relationship life, commit to working on your inner self-confidence and purpose in life, so that you can feel good about yourself and about your life. When you feel good about yourself and the direction in which you are steering your life, it will be easier to attract, approach, and date beautiful women.

Picking up women is not the right approach to dating. If "pick up women" is the mentality you are employing in your current dating and relationship life, you are likely to feel frustrated, since the "art" of "pick up" is never about exploring sexual, romantic, and emotional compatibility. It is about *using* women.

When you adopt a "pick up women" mentality, you are likely to feel unsure of your ability to attract and date beautiful women. You are also likely to feel very unlucky with women, even though you try so hard, simply because picking up women is about tricking them—into bed or into relationships—by presenting yourself as a quality man while you do not feel or believe you are one.

Consider the following scenario:

After deciding to start using Tinder to meet new women, you, a "nice guy" who is timid, introverted, and a bit unsure of yourself, quickly finds yourself in murky dating waters that you have to navigate in order to come out at the other end with an interesting woman that you can take out on a potential date.

You discover that:

- You have to figure out what to say and how to say it.

- You have to talk to women in a way that gets them to respond, all the while "appearing aloof and unconcerned," because modern dating advice for men says that this is what "gets women going."

- You have to decipher the signals a woman uses to communicate during online conversations and use these signals to create a lasting impression so that the conversation can lead into an actual date or relationship.

- You have to lead the conversation forward until it materializes into whatever you want—perhaps a date—which is something you do not feel innately capable of doing, because you find online and offline dating too complicated to navigate.

- You also discover that even though you are shy and reserved, you feel you have to "fake" being confident because the women you want normally go for self-assured, confident men, who know where they are heading in life.

In the end, because the dating process seems complex and marred with too many rules and regulations, you give up: not because you are incapable of finding, attracting, and then dating beautiful women, but because you cannot make sense of the modern dating process.

What to do instead: " date" yourself.

If you can relate to any of the above, you should not give up. Instead, you need to change how you approach dating in the modern world. You need to focus less on the women you want to date and more on becoming the best man you can be. You need to focus on becoming a strong man who knows what he wants, honestly communicates it, and is not afraid to go out and get it.

Instead of thinking about how to "pick up" women using cheesy conversation starters, you need to think about what you can do to become the kind of man women want to be with and the kind of man women find attractive and want to approach. Fortunately, for you, doing this is not too difficult if you are willing to "date" yourself before you start dating anyone else.

Dating yourself is about discovering your true self, who you are and what you want in life, the kind of relationships you want, and the qualities you hold dear in a mate. It is about working on yourself long before you start dating, so that when you do start, you are confident, sure of your immense value as a man, and thus able to attract the women you want—interesting women you connect with.

Without having this element in place, without cultivating a strong sense of self—an immutable sense of self-confidence—and without being happy and content with the person you are right now (or the man you are becoming), your chances of attracting a high value woman are very slim.

If you do not know how to become a self-confident, alpha male, do not worry too much about it, because showing you how to become such a man is the purpose of this guide.

Section 2:

Doing the Hard Work First –

How to Become a Confident, Alpha Male That Women Find Irresistible

The various chapters that make up this section shall decipher important issues—like why confidence is the secret to success in dating for you and what it means to be confident. You will also learn what the "alpha male" mentality is and how to adopt it; how to work on yourself so that you become more confident and attractive; and various other topics that, together, should help you become more self-assured.

As mentioned earlier, do not skip reading this section, because the various things we shall discuss in the chapters that make up this section will be fundamental to your ability to implement the dating advice found in the next section of the book.

In the introductory part of this guide, we talked a lot about confidence and it being the secret to dating for men. It is therefore only fair that we start this section by explaining what it means to be a confident man, why being one is important, and what you can do to become confident and therefore attractive to women.

Chapter 1: Confidence – What It Means to You, Why It's the Secret to Dating Success, and How to Cultivate It

In this chapter, we are going to discuss the oft-confusing topic of confidence, why it is the secret to success, and more importantly, how to develop it so that you become more self-assured and therefore more attractive to women.

Confidence 101: What It Means to You

If you are a big fan of the Marvel Cinematic Universe, you have probably seen the movie *Captain America: The First Avenger* (2011).

The movie has a scene where, before joining the army and becoming the mighty "Captain America," we see Steve Rogers in a movie theater watching an army-recruitment video.

As Steve keenly watches "little Timmy" do his part for the war effort by collecting scrap metal, a loud "jerk" in the audience starts interrupting and disrespecting the men giving up their lives to serve the United States of America by saying things like: "Who cares?" and "Play the movie already!"

Steve quietly asks the "jerk" to, "... show some respect," and continues watching the video of the war efforts keenly. The man makes a snide sound, and before long, he is disrespecting the sacrifice of those joining the army again by saying things like "let's go," "get on with it," and "hey, just start the cartoon already."

At that point, without being wholly aware of who is disrespecting the war effort because the auditorium is dark, a visibly annoyed Steve Rogers says to the man, "... shut up." At this, the huge "jerk" stands up and towers over Steve, clearly angry at the comment to "shut up," and the scene fades to one where the big man is pummeling Steve Rogers to the ground with mighty punches to the head one after the other.

No matter how hard the "jerk" hits him, Steve keeps getting back up, fists at the ready—even though he is not landing any punches on the big man. Clearly surprised by the smaller man's ability to get back up after every heavy punch, the big "jerk" says, "You just don't know when to give up, do you?" to which Steve replies, "I can do this all day."

You are probably wondering to yourself, what does this have to do with anything—particularly with me becoming great at attracting and meeting women?

The Steve Rogers scene described above has everything (or at least a lot) to do with what it takes to unlock the secrets to meeting new people and attracting women by being a confident alpha male.

Here is why; but first, use the following link to watch the scene—you can watch it up to the end of the fight scene when Bucky Barnes rescues Steve from the "jerk."

https://bit.ly/2Qi7Yqc (*Captain America: The First Avenger.* Film. United States: Joe Johnston, 2011.)

If you had to guess, what would you give as a reason for why Steve was the only person in the movie theater to say something about the "jerk's" disrespectful demeanor toward the war effort?

Continuing with this, during the fight scene, we see Steve continuously making a comeback after each heavy fist to the noggin. If you had to guess, what would you give as the reason for his comeback? More importantly, even though he is taking a rough beating, why does he say, "I can do this all day?"

Make a wild guess.

You guessed right: deep self-belief and courage, what we can also refer to as masculine confidence, dogged determination, or an alpha male mentality.

First, Steve tells the loud jerk to shut up because he believes in what is right, which in this case is supporting the army, and that he should be ready to stand up for it; even though he is too small and too sickly to actually join the war effort.

Second, when the screen cuts to the fight scene, Steve continuously bounces back from each punch and says, "I can do this all day" because he believes in himself and in standing up for what he wants, which in this case is teaching the jerk a lesson: *do not disrespect the army!*

This strong belief in himself precedes him undergoing the chemical treatment that turns meekly Steve Rogers into the well-built Captain America. We would in fact be right if we said that Steve did not become Captain America because he underwent the treatment, but because of his firm belief in himself and in something "bigger," he was *always* Captain America.

This firm belief in himself and in the war effort is the reason why Steve finally gets a chance to join the Strategic Scientific Reserve. It is also the reason why even though the physical training is mind-numbingly difficult, and even though he struggles to keep up with the other well-built trainees, Steve is the person selected to become "the first in a new breed of super soldiers."

Although fictional, this story can teach you a lot about meeting and attracting women. The underlying sentiments of your aims and the aims of Steve Rogers are very similar. You both have a goal; yours is to become better at attracting and interacting with women, Steve's goal was to serve his country in any capacity.

Steve Rogers did not become Captain America because he was strong; on the contrary, because he was "strong of spirit," and a "confident" man, he was Captain America long before his chemical transformation. The simple truth is that "Captain America" is about more than an outer appearance, it is a spirit of believing in oneself and in something bigger.

To become better at attracting and interacting with women, you need to become like Steve Rogers: you need to believe in yourself and in your purpose so strongly that no matter what—no matter how many metaphorical "punches" to the face you take—like Steve, you will say, "I can do this all day."

Self-confidence is the secret not just to dating and relationship success, but success in all areas of your life in general. When, like Steve, you believe in yourself so strongly that no challenge seems too big, you become capable of surmounting any odds stacked against you; including being shy, or a "nice guy."

Self-confidence as the secret to dating and relationship success is usually a murky topic, because confidence means different things to different people.

Before we discuss how to cultivate a strong sense of self-confidence that helps you attract women, let us briefly talk about what self-confidence means to you—or what it should start meaning to you as you read this guide and implement what you learn.

What manly confidence means to you.

"Once we believe in ourselves, we can risk curiosity, wonder, spontaneous delight, or any experience that reveals the human spirit."

 −E.E. Cummings

If you gather ten women for a pop-up survey, nine of them will tell you that confidence is the trait they find most attractive in a man, which is why it makes sense that: "be confident" is common advice in men's dating blogs and books.

Unfortunately, when dating "gurus" advise you to "be confident," they often fail to define what they mean by that, and what confidence should mean to you. As a result, the advice ends up being frustrating and unactionable because confidence can mean many things— especially when it comes to its application in dating and relationships.

Let us define what confidence means:

The best definition of confidence the (noun) comes from **kidshealth.org**. The platform describes confidence as follows:

> Confidence means feeling sure of yourself and of your abilities, not in an arrogant way, but in a realistic, secure way. Confidence is not about feeling superior to others. It is a quiet inner knowledge that you are capable and enough. Confident people: feel secure rather than insecure.

We can pin our understanding of confidence for this guidebook to this definition because it encompasses everything confidence should mean to you. Every time you come across the phrase "be confident" in various parts of this book, remember that this means that you should have faith in yourself —or be sure of yourself—as you approach and interact with women and new people.

It also means you should believe in your ability to approach anyone—even the most beautiful woman you have ever seen—and carry on an interesting conversation; at the very least, it means you should believe that you are capable of improving your dating skills.

Adopting this definition and view toward confidence will help ensure that you believe in your limitless ability and potential to improve areas of your life where you feel incapable: such as starting conversations with women, displaying confident body language, et cetera.

Now that you know what the noun confidence means, let us take this definition a bit deeper.

Confidence is ...

In dating—and indeed in general life—confidence is less about "appearing" outwardly confident and more about cultivating an internal belief in yourself and in your abilities; it is about believing that if you put your mind and energy into it, you can achieve your goals and become the man you want to be.

Do not mistake this to mean mannerisms are not important because they are. As a matter of fact, how you carry yourself is very important and we shall discuss it at length later in the book. However, what you believe about yourself is more important because when your faith in yourself is strong, it is likely to manifest as a confident demeanor. On the other hand, when you have no faith in yourself, you are likely to be shy and timid, and it is likely to show in your behavior and demeanor as well.

Even if you lack confidence in some areas of your life, if you *believe* you are capable, confidence is something you can learn or acquire and sharpen until your belief in yourself is resolute.

Additionally, we can consider confidence to be an attitude. When we say a man is confident, what we truly mean is that the man in question has a certain way about him, a certain swagger that shows he believes in himself and that he has faith in his abilities.

Confidence as an attitude is not about what you may have going for you such as money, nice clothes, good looks, et cetera. Like Steve Rogers, you may be the smallest man in the room and have a sense of confidence that shames that of the biggest man you know. Money, for example, is nice to have, but when a man who lacks self-confidence has this or other superficial attributes, the resulting character traits are usually arrogance and a cocky demeanor.

It is also fundamentally important to mention here that being confident does not mean being cocky or arrogant and you should not confuse these character traits. Unlike cockiness and arrogance, confidence is subtle. It does not announce itself loudly verbally, nor is it a shove-it-in-your-face type of character trait.

Because it comes from an inner sense of conviction and security in oneself; confidence—unlike cockiness and arrogance—has nothing to do with being raucous, pompous, showy (showing off), or even feeling superior. In fact, any man you see displaying these character traits is internally insecure and doing a bad job at faking outward confidence.

Confidence, especially in dating and relationships, is not condescending or patronizing; it is not about showing off what you have or believing that women respond better to boasting and bragging about money, your amazing job, expensive suits, or anything materialistic.

Yes, a small, *very* marginal portion of women may respond to such behavior, but chances are high that if your intention is to attract and date a high quality woman, showing off, boasting, or being arrogant will turn her off faster than you can say "abracadabra."

Unlike arrogance and cockiness, manly confidence is subtly attractive and very easy to discern, which is why when you cultivate it, women—and other people—will feel naturally attracted to you without you having to show off your latest expensive "acquisition," or even say a word. This is because when you have confidence, you project a radiance of self-assuredness, out of which, you display open and attractive body language that shows you are not wallowing in self-pity or stewing in the fear of failure or rejection, and are instead sure that you are a valuable and capable man.

Arrogance and cockiness are both about a faked "outward" expression of confidence. When you feel good about yourself and your inner capabilities, several things including your demeanor, the challenges you are willing to undertake, and your capacity for resilience all change for the better.

To help you gain a deeper understanding of what confidence means—or should mean to you now—so that you know exactly what you should aim to cultivate, here are a few pointers:

True confidence is owning and accepting.

It is very easy to assume that because confidence is a strong belief in yourself and in your capabilities, it also means overlooking your faults and shortcomings as a man. That is *not* the case.

Like most humans, confident men have plenty of insecurities, shortcomings, faults, and flaws. The only difference between these alpha males and, say, shy or arrogant men, is that instead of hiding or masking these insecurities and flaws in attitudes such as boasting, showing off, rowdiness, timidity, et cetera, confident men accept these faults and flaws. This is because these men understand that the only way to become better men is to accept these insecurities and flaws, so that they can start working on themselves.

Confidence is not—and never has been—about hiding your insecurities and flaws or masking your true, authentic identity in another one; only weak men lacking confidence do that. Confidence has always been and will continue to be about having an intimate awareness of who you are and what you believe you are capable of doing. Above that, confidence is about challenging any beliefs that may lead you into thinking you are not or *cannot* be good at something, such as talking to women or strangers, no matter how much you work at it.

When you own up to your insecurities, flaws and faults, and accept them, can you guess what happens?

First, because you become self-aware, it is easier to cultivate a deeper sense of self-belief in the things you know you are good at; second, by being aware of the insecurities, flaws, and beliefs that may be keeping you from being the best man you can be, working on your shortcomings becomes relatively easier.

For instance, when you accept (instead of denying and trying to hide) the fact that you are shy, timid, and not great at—or even afraid of—starting conversations with beautiful women, your mindset shifts from: "I don't have a problem," to one of: "I accept this about myself. What can I do to improve as a person?"

While this mindset shift seems simple, the inner changes in self-belief that it instigates will prove invaluable as you work toward mastering your dating and relationship life. Moreover, women consider a man who accepts his insecurities, flaws, and shortcomings, to be a "catch." This is because doing so is a sign of emotional intelligence or maturity, a trait that most women (secretly) want in their mates.

The other important thing that happens when you get into the habit of owning up to and accepting your faults, is that it humbles you, which keeps you from developing a grandiose sense of self-belief. This is because accepting your flaws helps you to realize that you are imperfect and that it is okay to be so. You do not need to pretend you are perfect to attract women, or to become someone you are not to strike-up and maintain conversations with new people and beautiful women.

Being candid—to yourself mostly—about your insecurities and shortcomings as a person frees you and opens you up to the realization that the women you want to attract and approach have their individual insecurities, shortcomings, and flaws, because as it is, no human is perfect. This lets you be vulnerable with these women, because if we are all humans—and thus imperfect—then there is no need to hide our insecurities or to be fearful or even anxious of them. This is because we know that when it comes to a beautiful woman, underneath that beauty—no matter how otherworldly it may be—is a flawed human being, just like us.

Additionally, when you acknowledge, own up to, and accept your flaws, faults, and shortcomings, it helps you realize that the only way to get better at anything is to start by embracing your authentic self *before* you start working on improving this self.

This is foundationally important, because when you do not feel the need to hide your authentic self behind an arrogant or cocky demeanor, you can connect with women who like you for who you are, which should be your ultimate goal.

In fact, and as mentioned earlier, if you notice a man—or woman for that matter—acting arrogant and cocky, it is because this person is working hard to hide their insecurities.

Hiding your insecurities should not be your aim—especially if you want to achieve success in your dating life, because if you hide your authentic self behind a fake demeanor, you will attract the "wrong" women. Chances are also high that the women you want to attract will see through it and consider you deceptive. Guess what, no woman wants to date or fall in love with a deceptive man.

Because you are committed to improving yourself—self-improvement is why you are reading this book—you have probably read plenty of self-confidence books and posts that say, "fake it until you make it," which means you should *fake* being confident until this fake confidence takes root in your psyche and you start *feeling* confident.

There is nothing wrong with this advice and if you feel immensely devoid of inner confidence, you should fake confident body language until you start feeling confident naturally. Doing so will greatly help you develop a spark of inner self-belief that, when fanned, will develop into a self-confidence inferno.

However, it is important to note that when dating and relationship experts advise you to, "fake being confident until you start feeling confident" they do not explicitly mean you should show your confidence outwardly by shoving it in other people's faces; this is arrogance, not confidence.

What these experts actually mean is that you should embrace your authentic self, which as we have noted, starts with owning up to and accepting your flaws and faults, so that you can be vulnerable (human) and allow your confidence to shine through subtly in your demeanor.

Confidence vs. arrogance: how to tell the difference.

The line between true confidence and arrogance (or cockiness) is razor thin. As a man who is looking to increase the former while keeping the latter in check, you need to understand this and internalize the core differences between the two, so that you have a firm idea of what it means to be truly confident, as opposed to being arrogant and cocky. Arrogance and cockiness are unattractive traits that women (and people in general) do not find endearing.

As mentioned earlier, confidence is having intimate knowledge of who you are and wholeheartedly accepting the man you are—improving elements of your self as necessary. On the other hand, as the actress Milena Markovna "Mila" Kunis notes: "Cockiness is knowing who you are and pushing it down everyone's throat."

When you are confident, you are comfortable with who you are and therefore do not feel the need to shove it down people's throats by telling everyone how you did X, accomplished Y—and perhaps how much money you earned last quarter or how "fat" your bank account is right now.

When you are truly confident, you understand that even though you embrace your authentic self and are comfortable in your skin—a fact that shows subtly in your demeanor—you do not need to shove it in people's faces because you are also human and therefore, you have flaws that you need to work on in order to improve.

When you are cocky, arrogant, and overconfident, even though you may be comfortable in your skin, you have a distorted view of yourself (and of others) because you are likely to believe that you are the perfect human specimen.

Because of this belief, you are likely to be self-centered, a person who never shies away from a chance to talk about how great you are, or how amazing your life is. Such an attitude is likely to turn off women because one of the things women respond immensely well to is a "humble man" who knows when to shut up, what to share with others, and what to keep to himself.

Think of it as follows:

If you are the kind of man who constantly regales others with tales of your achievements and greatness, every high-quality woman you know will display a lot of angst over dating you. This is because she will be fearful that you dating—and perhaps bedding—her will be one of the conquests you share with your "boys" in proclamation of "how great you are with women." No woman wants to feel like a trophy or sexual conquest.

More importantly, unlike confidence that is subtle and has a quietly attractive demeanor, arrogance is loud and often leaves others feel inferior. As you can imagine, when you make the women you want to attract and date feel inferior, they are likely to want to keep their distance, which is likely to narrow your dating pool and limit your ability to achieve success in your dating and relationship life.

Another vital difference between confidence and arrogance is this: according to Robert Glatter, M.D., when you develop arrogance or become overconfident, you are likely to "talk the talk but not walk the walk." For instance, you are likely to give into the temptation to exaggerate your accomplishments in a bid to awe others.

On the other hand, when you are genuinely confident, you are likely to talk less about yourself and are instead likely to let your work or actions speak the loudest for you, something women find immensely sexy and attractive.

When you get into the habit of hiding your flaws, you are also likely to get into the habit of talking a good game that you cannot back up with tangible skills or principles, something that is likely to work against you improving your dating and relationship life.

Instead, you need to embrace your authentic self so that you can attract someone who accepts you for who you are; so if you notice that your insecurities and beliefs are limiting your success in dating, you should embark on working on them.

Knowing who you are and being proud of it.

This point is very important to note, not just because it builds upon the last one, but also because without knowing who you are and then accepting this person, it is impossible to find, attract, and then date the kind of woman you want and deserve.

Do you know why?

First, because before you start dating—or at the very least *looking* for potential dates—the first thing you need to do is have a clear idea of what you want.

Is your intention to date casually, find love, start a long-term relationship, et cetera? To determine any of these things, you need to introspect, find out who you are, and then accept this person wholeheartedly—even if you intend to embark on self-development.

Second, one of the prerequisites to dating success is to define the kind of woman you want; not from a physical perspective—although physique is an important consideration—but from a character trait perspective.

Do you want to meet a woman who likes hiking, who reads, who is positive, who is quiet, caring, gentle, et cetera, who does X or Y?

Determining this is fundamentally important to your success in the dating scene. This is because as we have noted, just as money attracts money, high quality women attract high quality men, and if you want to attract a woman who has specific character traits, you need to embody those character traits first, which is impossible to do if you do not know who you are.

Moreover, when you embark on the journey to self-awareness, which is what knowing and accepting yourself is truly about, it becomes easier to own up to and accept your flaws and faults, and as we have said, when you adopt the habit of accepting your flaws, you are unlikely to practice self-grandiosity or arrogance.

Being vulnerable.

"I understand now that the vulnerability I've always felt is the greatest strength a person can have. You cannot experience life without feeling life. What I've learned is that being vulnerable to somebody you love is not a weakness, it's a strength."

—Elisabeth Shue

Being confident is never about not showing weakness. If anything, being vulnerable is in line with the various points we have mentioned in this section of the guide.

Confidence is not something you feel or have because you are perfectly flawless; on the contrary.

When you are confident and therefore at peace with the person you are, hiding your authentic self is the last thing you are likely to want to do. In fact, when you are truly confident, you are likely to be very aware of your insecurities and limiting beliefs.

Moreover, when you are not confident enough to be vulnerable and "imperfectly you" with the women you want to attract and date, you will be fooling yourself and these women because since you are hiding your "true self." These women will not fall in love with the real you but with the fake you. Such deception does not create the best foundation, irrespective of what kind of relationship you have in mind.

Being truly confident is about being vulnerable, because when you are confident yet vulnerable, you open yourself up to being truly compassionate. Being confident in this way also allows you to be openly there for yourself and for others; without letting sentiments such as "showing vulnerability makes me weak" stop you from building the courage to own up to your flaws and shortcomings.

As you were reading this subsection, you may have wondered to yourself, "Why do I need self-confidence in order to be successful in dating? It's not like dating is a make-or-break interview for my dream job." But, as you will realize, it is the key to your dating success.

Why Self-Confidence is the Secret to Dating Success

"As soon as you trust yourself, you will know how to live."

–Johann Wolfgang von Goethe

Can we be brutally honest for a moment? You can take it, right?

If you are not confident, you will not achieve success in your dating and relationship life. It truly is that simple and there really are no two ways about it.

The good thing though is that even if you consider yourself a nice, shy, and complacent man, you can do something to become more confident with women, but before we get to that, let us delve a bit deeper into why self-confidence is the secret to an excellent dating and relationship life.

Let us start at the most basic reason why:

It creates positive self-perception.

For the purpose of this guide, we have defined confidence (also self-confidence) as a firm belief in your value, in yourself, and in your abilities.

The essence of this definition is that self-confidence is about self-perception, which is of fundamental importance because *what you think about yourself* greatly influences how you approach everything—including dating and relationships.

If you are a bit skeptical about this fact, consider this:

The unconfident man approach to dating and courtship.

For a moment, let us assume you like this one woman; let us call her Jane. You like Jane a lot and you believe she is the "one," the perfect woman for you. However, you are shy, insecure, timid, and your self-belief or self-confidence is super low.

Because your self-belief is extremely low, your self-perception is negative, which is why even though you want nothing more than to be with Jane for the rest of your life, you never gather the courage to walk up to her. In fact, every time you think of walking up to her to say hello and to introduce yourself, you always talk yourself out of it. This is because you do not believe in yourself or your deservedness of Jane because "she is the most beautiful and amazing woman" you know and therefore out of your league.

Because of your insecurities, you nurture unprofessed loved for Jane for years and watch as she dates this or that man—and guess what? She finally walks down the aisle with a man that is not you. It shatters your heart and because Jane was "the one," you swear off women because it leads to heartache and pain.

While this narrative is fictional, when you lack self-confidence, such scenarios are likely to become a common occurrence in your dating and relationship life. This is because when you lack self-confidence, you have a poor self-perception—something that is likely to affect how you go about doing everything in your life, including approaching the woman of your dreams.

When you lack confidence and then your self-criticism flares up, which it perhaps often does; every time you think about approaching a woman, you are likely to buy into what this critical voice tells you.

For example, when your confidence is low, your inner dialogue is likely to be negative too, because you have no self-belief. When negativity and self-criticism become your default mode of thinking, it limits your potential and keeps you from being your authentic self.

Moreover, a negative inner monologue turns you into a skeptic and pessimistic person. Because of this, every time you think of walking up to a woman you would like to introduce yourself to and know with dating in mind, you are likely to think up all the reasons why she is too good for you or why you do not deserve her.

As opposed to the above, when you believe in yourself and your self-confidence is high, your inner monologues are likely to be largely positive. Because you have a high—not grandiose—sense of self, you are likely to believe that you deserve good things in life, which is why when you see a beautiful woman you would like to know, you are likely to look for all the reasons why you deserve her and why she deserves to have you as her man.

Again, this change in perspective seems miniscule and non-influential, but the number of men who have talked themselves out of approaching a woman with whom they can start an amazing relationship is huge—if you are shy and timid, you are likely to relate to this.

Now let us talk about another adjacent reason why confidence is essential to your dating and relationship life:

It opens you up to meeting new people.

Confidence is the secret to your dating success because being confident gives you the courage to meet new people.

Think of it this way: assume you are walking down the street, or are at a bar, or the park, et cetera. and you see a woman that catches your fancy. Like most men, you are likely to think to yourself: "She sure is gorgeous. Well, she probably has a boyfriend."

There's nothing wrong with thinking such a thought; it is in fact normal to rationalize an inability to approach new people by saying things such as, "I don't have time to talk to her right now," or "I don't know what to say," "She will reject me," et cetera.

However, to enhance your chances of finding an ideal mate— irrespective of your dating or relationship intentions—such an attitude is not beneficial. It shall in fact keep you from meeting new women who have the potential to turn into amazing dates and mates.

Most men usually fail to have amazing dating and relationship lives simply because they have closed themselves off to meeting new people. This is because most men who lack confidence and self-belief often talk themselves out of approaching or talking to the women they find attractive and people they find interesting. Confidence is the secret to dating and relationship success because it changes this dynamic.

When you are self-confident and self-assured, it opens you up to meeting new people, because when you see a woman you consider beautiful and would like to talk to and know, instead of coming up with excuses for why you should not do it, you push past these reasons and embrace the discomfort. This allows you to challenge yourself into starting a conversation and out of that, your chances of starting amazing courtships and relationships improve significantly.

Additionally, when you are self-assured, you are more likely to put yourself out there because you understand that rejection is never about you as a person; it is usually about your approach or misaligned interests.

Confidence is about taking chances. When you have it in spades, taking chances by talking to women and new people becomes easier. Confidence is the secret to dating and relationship success, because when you are confident, it shows in your demeanor and body language. When your body language is positive, it attracts others and enhances your chances of meeting new people, because open and confident body language cues such as a friendly smile and curious eye contact are very attractive and endearing.

Helps you overcome anxiety and fear.

A primary reason why self-confidence is the secret to dating success is that it helps you overcome fear and anxiety. This is because when you feel self-assured, you are likely to practice positive self-talk.

This is very important because when your negative inner critic fires up and says things such as, "She is out of your league," "She will reject you," or "You will fail," you can use the positive self-talk to quell and counter these thoughts with positive ones, such as: "I deserve to be with a woman as beautiful as she is," "I am interesting as a person and I have a lot to offer the right woman," or "If I say hello, I might make a new friend or romantic connection," et cetera.

When you can talk to yourself in such a positive manner, it becomes easier to detach from your thoughts, reconnect with the present moment, and then take action by respectfully approaching the woman you want.

Helps you cultivate emotional resiliency.

If you take a moment to think about why you never take action when you see a woman you would like to approach, talk to, know, and perhaps start a relationship with, you will quickly realize that the fear of rejection and failure is the primary reason. Confidence takes care of this.

When you are confident and self-assured, in addition to enhancing your ability to challenge negative self-talk and reframe it positively, you are also equipped with essential emotional coping skills and strategies that make it easier to handle challenges and overcome setbacks.

For instance, being self-assured does not mean that women will stop rejecting you altogether or reject you less; they will. The only difference is that because you are self-assured and confident in your value as a man, you will not take this to heart so much that it ruins your self-esteem. Instead, you shall pass it off as "misaligned intention," which will help keep the fear of rejection or failure from crippling your ability to take action toward the things you want.

Moreover, confidence opens you up to new experiences, which is essential to meeting new people—especially women—because when you are willing to try new things, you also open yourself up to growth opportunities in all areas of your life; including your dating and relationship life.

As you have seen from the four points above, confidence is indeed the secret to dating and therefore, to achieve success in your dating and relationship life, you need to cultivate it as a matter of importance.

Let us now discuss various practical strategies and habits you can use to cultivate deeper self-assuredness.

Concrete Strategies and Habits to Help You Grow and Foster Inner Self-Confidence

In this subsection, we are going to outline various practical strategies and habits you can adopt to become more self-confident and self-assured.

Cultivate internal and external confidence.

Self-confidence falls into two primary categories: internal and external self-confidence. Both are very important and here is how to cultivate both.

How to cultivate external confidence.

From a very broad perspective, this kind of confidence is important because it comes from feeling capable of doing a task or activity competently or successfully.

Consider the following scenario:

When you do not know what to say to women, you are likely to feel very nervous and lack confidence, and because you do not feel competent at having conversations, you are likely to feel inadequate and insecure. On the other hand, when you know what to do, say, or how to complete a certain task—such as starting an interesting online conversation—you are likely to feel self-assured and capable.

Also called "situational confidence," external self-confidence is domain specific, in the sense that you feel capable of doing some things well and incapable of doing others. This is why you may be the CEO of your company but still unable to talk to women: because you have competence in one area and feel that you lack confidence in another.

Situational confidence is very easy to cultivate. Do you know why? Because this kind of confidence comes from practice, and therefore, the more you practice something, the better you become at it, and the more competent you feel.

To cultivate situational confidence with women, you only need to do one thing: start approaching and *talking* to women. No matter how shy or bad at it you are, just start! Yes, you will suck at it at first, and women will reject you many times over, but with every trial and with every rejection, you will callous your mind to rejection and build emotional resiliency.

> "Until you experience hardships like abuse and bullying, failures and disappointments, your mind will remain soft and exposed. Life experience, especially negative experiences, help callous the mind."
>
> —David Goggins

More importantly, the more you put yourself out there, and the more chances you take, the more confident you will feel and the better you will become at approaching women and starting conversations with new people, which will significantly improve your ability to meet, attract, and date the woman of your dreams.

Here are additional practical strategies and habits you can use to cultivate external self-confidence:

- **Treat every situation as a learning experience.** Whenever you meet a beautiful woman you would like to talk to and perhaps date, no matter how shy or bad at talking to women you are, treat this as a learning opportunity and take a chance, because as mentioned earlier, situational confidence is a result of experience.

- **Practice self-awareness so that you can challenge your inner talk.** As mentioned, most men shy away from talking to the women of their dreams because their negative inner self-talk stops them from taking chances. You can overcome this by challenging these thoughts. When you meet a woman you would like to date, connect with the present moment so that you can become aware of the conversations happening in your mind, and should you notice negative self-talk, you can question and challenge its authenticity.

- **Develop specific interpersonal skills.** External confidence comes from feeling competent at doing certain contextual things. For instance, if you have your driver's license and drive frequently, you are confident in your driving skills. You should apply the same mentality to dating and approaching women, by making the decision to get started on developing specific interpersonal skills. Here, think of the interpersonal areas you feel least confident in and then seek to develop these specific skills through practice. For instance, if you think you are bad at approaching women and starting conversations, concentrate on improving this skill. If you feel you are incapable of turning a one-off conversation into a date, concentrate on building this skill. The more competent you become at specific interpersonal abilities, the more confident you shall feel in your ability to attract the woman of your dreams.

- **Crave and embrace discomfort.** To develop situational confidence, you need to embrace discomfort, because to develop this kind of confidence, you have to put yourself "out there" and seek new experiences. Remember that emotional resiliency—or what we called "callousing your mind"—does not come easy or overnight; it comes from constantly embracing discomfort and working with it, which can only be possible if you are willing to do things that make you feel uncomfortable. Whenever you notice an attractive woman you would like to talk to, do not overthink it, just do it. The more you think about it, the higher the chances are of you talking yourself out of taking action. To become more comfortable with being uncomfortable, start small. For instance, when you see a woman you like, compel yourself to say a simple "hello." Then the next time you see another woman you find attractive, say "hello" and follow it up with some small talk. If you keep doing this, you will train your mind to embrace discomfort and you will develop the confidence you need to become better at approaching woman for dating purposes.

• **Work toward mastery.** No matter how terrible you think you are at specific areas of interpersonal relations with women, set your eyes on mastery. When you do this, your mindset shall shift to one of embracing challenges and learning from discomfort.

The most important thing to remember about external or situational confidence is that it develops out of feeling competent. You can therefore develop it in different areas of your dating life by becoming more aware of the areas where you feel incompetent and then deliberately seeking out situations that help you cultivate competence in these areas. The more you practice, the better you shall become and the more confident and self-assured you shall feel.

How to cultivate internal confidence.

Internal confidence is a choice. This kind of confidence is very important because you can have it irrespective of your competence level.

Think of it this way:

Even though you may not be competent at talking with women, simply believing you are good at it can significantly increase your chances of talking to women you would like to date.

Even though both types of confidence are important, of the two, internal self-confidence—or what we call "core" self-confidence—is more important because it relates to what you think about yourself. If you believe you are confident with women, whether you are bad at being with women or not will not matter because your inner self-belief and conviction will render you willing to approach and talk to new women.

A study published by the University of California-Berkeley noted that, "... those who truly believe in their ability to succeed are the ones who end up being the most successful at doing just that." The implication of this is that if you strongly believe you are capable of attracting the woman of your dreams, you shall succeed at it—it may take a while, but because you believe in yourself, you will not give up until you do. Like Steve Rogers, your mindset shall be "I can do this all day."

The best way to increase your inner confidence is to work on your self-belief.

You can use a number of strategies to do this:

• **Challenge your beliefs.** Spend a small portion of your day (15-30 minutes should be enough) engaged in self-reflection. More specifically, since your intention is to improve your dating and relationship skills and life, spend some of this "me" time thinking about the various things you believe about your ability to attract, talk to, and date beautiful and interesting women. Think deeply about whether your beliefs are complementary or incompatible with the kind of dating and relationship life you want. If they are not, interrogate them and look for contradictory evidence. The more you challenge your negative beliefs, the easier it is to develop inner conviction in your ability to attract the kind of woman you deserve and want in your life.

• **Visualize success with women.** Visualization is a new-age science strategy that calls on you to use your mind to imagine an ideal scenario. For instance, if you believe you are not good at approaching women and starting conversations, visualization asks you to picture yourself as being successful at this undertaking. Visualization is powerful because it gives your subconscious mind contradicting "evidence." When you visualize yourself as a confident man who is capable of approaching women and starting conversations, the subconscious mind cannot tell the difference between make believe and reality, and it will take this to mean you are great at approaching and talking to women.

• **Use affirmations.** To build core self-confidence, you need to build inner conviction; you need to believe you are capable, worthy, and deserving of dating amazing women. Affirmations can help you do that. An affirmation is a statement you repeat deliberately with the intention of imbedding it and the attendant belief into your subconscious mind. Affirmations are powerful because they help you to adopt a new way of viewing yourself. For instance, when you loudly repeat an affirmation such as "I am good at approaching and talking to women," you eventually start believing this affirmation because the human mind eventually believes what you tell it (affirm) often. When you repeat this affirmation, your brain shall seek evidence to reinforce it.

• **Cultivate fear awareness.** If you consider yourself bad at talking to women, it is probably because you have related fears and insecurities. When it comes to approaching women, nothing is as crippling as the fear of rejection or failure, which is why to create internal confidence, you need to cultivate fear awareness—and then work toward uprooting your fears and insecurities. Rejection or failure is the most common fear in most men. This fear preys on your doubts, blows things out of proportion, and overwhelms you to the point of paralysis. For instance, when you see women you consider beautiful, you are likely to think things such as: "What if she rejects me?" "What if she says no?" or "What if people see her rejecting me and laugh at me?" Such fears are common. To become more internally confident, you need to cultivate awareness of these fears and then use strategies such as affirmations and visualization to uproot them from your psyche. Always remember that to become a confident man, you have to know what you want and then not be afraid to go out and get it—despite the risk of failure. You can overcome your fears by rehearsing worst-case scenarios of approaching women. Doing this will callous your mind and make you emotionally resilient to things such as rejection, embarrassment, et cetera, which will improve your self-belief and make you more willing and capable of approaching women and putting yourself out there.

The fundamental thing to remember about developing core confidence is that it comes from inner conviction: a deep belief in yourself and in your abilities. Any strategy or habit that helps you cultivate positive self-belief will help you develop internal self-belief.

Create a morning and evening routine.

Confidence is more than just feeling good about yourself: it's also feeling capable and in control of your life. While feeling in control of your life is a multi-pronged endeavor, creating a morning and evening routine is one of the most effective ways boost this feeling.

A morning and evening routine serves various purposes. First, it ensures that you get adequate sleep—because one of the things it calls for is sleeping and waking up at the same time.

You may be wondering, "What does getting adequate sleep have to do with confidence with women?" Well, **a study conducted on doctors and published on BMJ journals** noted that getting adequate sleep at night leads to increased feelings of wellbeing, better mood, higher energy levels, and enhanced confidence. The results of the study proved that when you get adequate sleep, you feel better about yourself (which is internal self-confidence).

Secondly, when you create an effective morning and evening routine, it helps you to internalize self-confidence as a practice. This is because when you wake up on time every day, it helps you to feel in control of your schedule and life, which makes you feel more competent and capable, and to develop self-discipline, the most important of all "masculine" character traits.

Your morning and evening routines can include a number of activities: such as exercising, personal grooming, meditation, and goal setting for the day in the morning; or reading, journaling, and introspecting in the evening. As you can see, these wellness-related habits can significantly help you feel more confident and in control of your life and of yourself.

Adopt an " alpha male" mindset in your daily life.

To become a "manly" man; a man who is confident, self-assured, and capable of approaching and talking to women, you need to adopt an "alpha male" mindset and make it the blueprint you use to live your life.

Because this is crucial to your success in dating and relationships, let us talk about it as a stand-alone topic:

Chapter 2: The Alpha Male Mindset – Attract Women by Bringing Out the Alpha Male within You

"Men should be busy with their mission and purpose in life, not sitting around waiting to spring into action to be a woman's therapist or digital pen pal when she gets bored."

—Coach Corey Wayne

To build inner and outer confidence, you need to adopt and embody the alpha male mindset. The aim of this chapter is to define what it means to be a modern alpha male, show you why being an alpha male will help you attract women and experience great success in your dating life, and then later, we shall look at how you can embody the alpha male mindset inside out.

Let us start by defining what an alpha male is and is not:

Myth Busting: What an Alpha Male is and is Not

The term alpha male became popular after the publication of L. David Mech's book, *The Wolf: The Ecology and Behavior of an Endangered Species.*

In the book, Mech notes that as it relates to social animals—and humans are social animals—the term "alpha male" denotes the leader of a social group; he goes on to note that in social animals, becoming the "alpha" takes a show of superior intelligence, physical strength, and aggressiveness.

This definition, about an alpha male being dominating, masculine, and competitive, is the old and worn out definition of what it means to be an "alpha male."

In the modern world, being an alpha male has nothing to do with being aggressive, dominating, chauvinistic, arrogant, close-minded, mean, or displaying any other trait you would expect an arrogant man to display. As mentioned earlier, developing such character traits is a sure way to turn off women.

Being an alpha male has nothing to do with being muscular or having a domineering posture. It has very little to do with being at the top of the hierarchy in your industry, having a "black card" and an overflowing bank account, feeling superior to other men in society, being handsome, or dating one model after the other, sometimes at the same time.

Before you misunderstand this: *yes,* most "alphas" are leaders in their industries; successful; and they have money, but these traits—being leaders at work or having money—are not the character traits that make these men alphas or so alluring to women.

In reality, being an alpha male is about being a valuable and purposeful man and as you can guess, to become a valuable and purposeful man, you have to know what you want so that you can be true and authentic to yourself.

Being an alpha male is about marrying your feminine and masculine energy, because you understand this is how to become emotionally intelligent, which means being emotionally vulnerable and brave, as well outwardly strong and unafraid of pursuing the things you want.

Being an alpha male is about being confident of what you are capable of, what you stand for as a man, and going for what you want; whether that is a specific woman, a career, a goal, a certain cause, et cetera. It is about being the leader of your own life—we call this having a purpose or direction in life—and being there to help, support, protect, stand up for, and lead the people that matter to you—family, friends that trust you, et cetera.

Being an alpha has nothing to do with being non-emotional. If that were the case, narcissistic men would be the truest embodiment of what it means to be true alpha men; we know better. Because being an alpha male is about emotional intelligence, which comes with being emotionally vulnerable and brave, it also means that narcissistic, arrogant men cannot be alphas because their sense of self-grandiosity diminishes their ability to show empathy, and therefore to practice emotional intelligence.

For this guide, whenever we use the term "alpha male," here is what that means and how you should embody that:

Being a true alpha male is about being in touch with your authentic self; it is about standing up for this authentic self, for what is right, and at the same time being sensitive to other people's rights and needs, which is emotional intelligence.

Being a true alpha male is about being sure of who you are and being comfortable with this person, while at the same time striving to be a better man than you were yesterday. We call this self-betterment and competing with yourself instead of with other men.

Being a true alpha male is about having the right mindset, a mindset of being supportive to yourself and your "clan," the people you care about, instead of being fiercely competitive so that you can have the biggest "slice of a meal."

We have mentioned that being a true alpha male is a mindset; this means alpha males think and behave a specific way.

Let us discuss that a bit more.

How Alpha Males Think, Act, and Key Alpha Male Traits

Since we have mentioned that being an alpha male is a mindset, let us cultivate a deeper understanding of what it means to be a true alpha male by looking at how alpha males think:

How alpha males think (and how that attracts women).

Because being a true alpha male is about knowing your authentic self and then being true to this self, it involves a specific thought process that differentiates alpha males from "beta," shy, and "nice guy" males.

A beta male is a man who is shy, demure, lacking confidence or a purpose, a man who does not know who he is or what he wants. Beta males are risk averse, which means even when they know what they want—which is very rare—they are usually unwilling to pursue the things they want, especially when the attached risk is bigger than they can handle.

On the other hand, most alpha males have a risk tolerant thought process, especially when the said risk leads to the things they want.

Take the following example:

Two men, one an alpha and one a beta, see a woman they want to date because both men think this woman could be the "one." Because the alpha male knows who he is, what he wants, and is not afraid to go after it despite any risk, he is likely to take a chance—even if it means a little personal discomfort or the chance of rejection.

On the other hand, because the beta male is more risk averse, the chances of rejection are likely to deter him from making a move. Instead of taking action, the beta male is likely to complain about how "sucky" his dating life is, or how he "cannot find love."

In most instances, beta males think about why they *should not* do something, while alpha males think about why they *should* do something.

This difference in thought process may seem miniscule but it makes all the difference, because when you are thinking about why you should not do something, your thought process is negative; when you are thinking about why you should do something, your thought process is positive and optimistic.

Having a positive or optimistic frame of mind is very foundational to success in all areas of your life because positive self-talk shows in your body as confident body language. When you display positive body language, women find you immensely attractive.

Losing face is an acceptable risk to an alpha male, because to him, the worst thing that can happen is a wasted opportunity or chance.

Because of being sure of what they want and not being afraid to pursue it, alpha males are bold and confident, something women often find irresistible. Because they have a positive thought process and their mindset is healthy, alpha males act a certain way that makes them immensely attractive to women.

Let us talk about that briefly:

How alpha males act (why women find it attractive and how to embody it).

Alpha males carry themselves in a very specific way: they display confident body language that is a result of inner self-assuredness and a healthy sense of self-belief.

Because they have an intuitive ability to read body language, women find alpha males' confident body language very attractive because, evolution-wise, women want to associate with men who know what they want and who are not afraid to pursue it.

Therefore, being a leader—in control of your own life, knowing what you want, and not being afraid to go after it—is a trait that the feminine energy easily recognizes and finds immensely attractive.

Alpha males have the following character traits that women find attractive and that you can embody to adapt the alpha male mentality:

1. Confident assertiveness.

Alpha males are assertive while betas are passive.

Alpha males also act assertively in the sense that they are not afraid to express their needs and desires or to voice their opinion even when their views do not align with what is popular, something every woman wants in a man because an assertive man is a man who knows how to lead and set boundaries.

Women want you to be an emotionally intelligent and assertive man because they understand that you will never be afraid of communicating—and effective communication is one of the character traits every woman wants in her mate/date—because they know when conflict arises, an alpha will not fidget around unsure of what to do. He will take deliberate action.

2. Comfortable with themselves.

Another key character trait that most women find irresistible is when a man is comfortable with himself, even as he works toward self-improvement.

When you are comfortable with yourself, it shows in how you carry yourself. Women find this very attractive because it shows self-assuredness and denotes a man who is brave enough to go after what he wants and is not afraid to protect what he loves, something all women want.

3. Collaboration.

Even though alpha males know what they want, why they want it, and are not afraid to do whatever it takes to get it, because they are not competitive—the only person they compete with is the person they were yesterday—they are collaborative, kind, and considerate toward others.

These superior character traits make them attractive to women because they illustrate a man who is respectful of himself and of others.

Unlike "nice guy" beta males whose primary motivation behind caring and collaborating is to get something in return—called "nice guy points" or external praise and recognition—alpha males are collaborative because they genuinely care about the wellbeing of the important people in their lives.

No woman wants to be with a man who does not know how to collaborate with others. In fact, all women want a man with whom they can build something great, which is why social media hashtags such as "relationshipgoals" are so popular with women.

Women find the ability to collaborate sexy because it shows you are a man who knows the value of compromise, the foundational element behind all successful courtships and romantic couplings.

Throughout this discussion, one of the things we have noted is that being a true alpha male is less about what you have and more about your mindset and thought process toward life in general—and dating in particular.

We have also done a fair job of explaining all the things alpha males are and are not, and some of the primary character traits that make them very attractive to women.

As you were reading this, you may have been thinking to yourself, "What are examples of alpha males that display the mindset and the character traits we have been discussing, and how can I emulate such men?"

Because being an alpha male is a mindset, alpha males come in all shapes and sizes, and they span different areas of society: such as the corporate world; the army; blue-collar work; Tech, et cetera. In general, any man who is confident and self-assured is an alpha male, irrespective of his current circumstances or inclination in life.

Examples of well-known alpha males.

We can consider fictional characters such as James Bond, Christian Grey, and Khal Drogo, and non-fictional men such as George Clooney, Jason Statham, and Dwayne "The Rock" Johnson to be "alphas." This is because if you look at the lives of these fictional and non-fictional men, you will notice that they embody the core alpha-male character traits we have discussed throughout this chapter of the guide.

Most of these men also have a very confident—but not arrogant—demeanor. If you interrogate their lives well, you will notice that they are famous and leaders in their areas—not just because they are handsome and strong, but also because they carry themselves in a specific way that is a result of inner confidence and a very specific mindset.

Take the example of Dwayne "The Rock" Johnson. There is no doubt that The Rock is muscular, strong, and wildly successful, the kind of man you would traditionally expect to be an alpha. These traits are however not what make him a true alpha.

What does is the fact that he has a very strong work ethic, which is why many Hollywood directors and producers love working with him. He speaks his mind and is not afraid to stand up for what he believes in; he is purposeful and driven, he is kind, compassionate, and humble, despite his success—a look at what he shares on social media will show you this.

Because of all this, he has achieved great acting and business success, and women (and some men) fall over themselves to be by his side.

If you examine the lives of all alpha males, you will notice similar character traits and demeanor: confident and positive verbal and body language as well as demeanor.

This should tell you that to become an alpha male, you should work on being confident from the inside out. The sub section: **concrete strategies and habits to help you grow and foster self-confidence** should help you start developing confidence from within.

To elevate this confidence so that alpha male characteristics become innate in your psyche and demeanor, adopt the body language cues discussed in the next chapter of this section.

Chapter 3: Body Language – How to Display Alpha Male Body Language and Attract Her Before You Speak

"What you do speaks so loud that I cannot hear what you say."

—Ralph Waldo Emerson

If you have read other "dating for men" books and blogs, you will have noted that most of these books immediately dive into showing you how to adopt positive or alpha male body language in order to improve your attractiveness, confidence, and dating life.

If you compare that to the format of this book, you will notice that we started by discussing how to cultivate inner confidence. We then moved on to what it means to be an alpha male before coming to this chapter, where we shall discuss how to display attractive, alpha male, confident body language before you approach women and new people.

This approach is very deliberate.

While "fake it until you make it" is good advice when it comes to a confident demeanor, to achieve great success with approaching women, this outer appearance needs to anchor to an alpha male mindset. Without cultivating this inner sense of self-worth and self-assuredness, outer displays of confidence won't help you become truly at ease with approaching women.

All a "faked" outer display of confidence will do is leave you feeling like an imposter—and guess what? When you feel like an imposter, it will show in your approach and in how you carry and conduct yourself around women too, which will all work against you.

Now that you are working to cultivate a healthy sense of self-confidence and self-esteem and seeing good results, we can start talking about how to elevate your confidence and masculine attractiveness.

Let us start by discussing the importance of body language and nonverbal communication:

Importance of Body Language and Nonverbal Communication

"Sixty percent of all human communication is nonverbal body language; thirty percent is your tone, so that means ninety percent of what you're saying ain't coming out of your mouth."

—Alex "Hitch" Hitchens

Body language and nonverbal communication is a great indicator of confidence, which is super important in dating and your relationship life.

Here is why:

Confident body language does not exist in a vacuum; it exists as an indicator of inner confidence. This is because, again, without a sense of inner confidence and conviction in who you are as a man, it becomes impossible to display genuinely confident body language or to use open and attractive nonverbal cues that attract people and women toward you. When you feel like an imposter, your demeanor is one of uncertainty.

Body language and nonverbal communication is important: especially in dating and relationships, because research has proven that a large portion of our communication is nonverbal.

In the 1960s, Albert Mehrabian conducted various research-based experiments that sought to determine what percentage of our communication depends on body language and nonverbal cues such as posture, intonation, gestures, body movements, and facial expressions—collectively called "nonverbal communication."

His results indicated that when discussing likes or dislikes, our interpretation of a person's message is dictated by this ratio: a **mere 7% is the actual words used, 38% is tone of voice, and 55% is nonverbal body language.** "Decoding of Inconsistent Communications." American Psychological Association https://www.psycnet.apa.org/doiLanding?doi=10.1037%2Fh0024532 (accessed January, 2020).

This means when you are saying one thing, perhaps to make you come off as confident, your body could be saying something completely different. This is not ideal because women have a very intuitive and well-developed ability to read body language, which means when you fake outer confidence without anchoring it to inner confidence, women will notice the deceit and it will turn them off.

> "Where body language conflicts with the words that are being said, the body language will usually be the more "truthful" in the sense of revealing true feelings."
>
> —Glen Wilson

Another reason why nonverbal cues and body language are so important in your dating life goes to the core of the aim of communication. The aim of body language and nonverbal communication is to share information. This is very important in dating and relationships because what you say with your body often speaks louder than what you say verbally, and because nonverbal communication makes up a large percentage of how we communicate, it plays a central role in attraction.

Think of it this way: how do you tell if a woman you are in the same room with would like you to approach her? You watch for body language and nonverbal cues such as an open smile and inviting body language. This can include engaging and communicative eye contact; touching her neck or playing with her hair; et cetera.

Body language and nonverbal communication is also important in dating and a great indicator of confidence, because the human mind does not decipher what you say verbally and what you say nonverbally as two distinct communication channels. Instead, the human mind relates what you are saying out loud to what you are saying with your body language.

This is very powerful in dating and in relationships because if you feel insecure, afraid, or anxious of approaching women and new people, this lack of self-assuredness will show in your body in one way or the other, no matter how much you try to hide it.

Now that you know the importance of body language and nonverbal communication and the role they play in attraction, dating, meeting new people, and creating worthwhile relationships, it is important to note that the first thing you ought to do is use **concrete strategies and habits to develop your inner self-confidence.** Doing this will help you become a strong, confident man who is sure of who he is, what he wants, and is most of all friendly and open to genuine connections with other people.

Once you feel internally confident, purposeful and because of it, in control of your life, your body language will change to mirror this conviction because your physiology changes depending on what you feel. For instance, if you feel passionate about a topic, cause, or aim, it will show off as passionate body language. If you feel internally confident, it will show off as confident body language.

Use these examples of strong body language and not-so-strong body language to determine your core body language:

Examples of Strong Body Language and Not-So-Strong Body Language

The following table outlines various examples of positive (strong) and negative (unattractive/not-so-strong) body language and nonverbal communication.

Keep in mind that you are always exhibiting body language and nonverbal signals subconsciously, and whether they appear positive or negative depends on your emotional state and your level of self-assuredness at the time.

Keep in mind too that the intention behind outlining positive and negative body language and nonverbal cues is to help you realize the kind of body language you display when meeting new people or women.

Positive Body Language	Negative Body Language
Relaxed posture: A relaxed posture says you are comfortable with who you are. Because relaxation also makes you more welcoming, it tells women and other people that you are open to new interaction.	**Closed off posture:** A closed off posture often indicates defensiveness, which is perhaps why, for instance, if you cross your hands across the chest, you will come off as anxious and unwelcoming.
A smile: Smiling is a welcoming nonverbal cue that says you are friendly and	**Frowning:** A frown can be a sign of many things, most of which are not attractive. For

welcoming.	example, it can say you are anxious about the space you are in, or that something is bothering you.
Comfortable eye contact: Maintaining friendly eye contact says you are interested, attentive, and that you are comfortable with who you are and not trying to hide anything.	**No eye contact:** Failing to maintain eye contact is a sign of insecurities, fear, anxiety, and in extreme cases, of insincerity.
Attentiveness: Attentiveness is a sign of confident body language because it shows interest in a woman or in other people. You can display attentiveness in a number of ways; such as friendly eye contact, open body language, et cetera.	**Lack of attentiveness:** If you have seen a woman you would like to attract, then not being attentive and aware communicates disinterest to her. Lack of attentiveness when you are communicating with other people also shows boredom or in some cases nervousness.
Taking up space: When you sit with an open and relaxed posture, you tend to take up a bit more space. This communicates that you are comfortable with who you are and that you are confident.	**Yielding body language:** You display yielding body language when you take up as little space as possible when even more is available to you. When you do this, it communicates discomfort, anxiety, a lack of self-esteem, and that you are closed off to new interaction, all of which turn off people—but women in particular.
Head held up: When you keep your head up, it shows you are confident, self-assured, and	**Slouched head:** Whether you are slouching to look at your phone or to fidget with a tissue,

ready to engage with the world around you.	not holding your head up says you are not open to new interactions or comfortable in the space you are in, both of which say you are feeling self-conscious and are therefore not feeling confident internally.
Relaxed facial expressions: Your face communicates a lot. When you adopt relaxed facial expressions, it is more attractive and communicates that you are open to meeting new people. Relaxed facial expressions also communicate comfort. An open smile, which is a sign of relaxed body language, is especially attractive and can draw in women: particularly when you smile because you feel good deep within.	**Tensed facial expressions:** When you display tensed facial reactions, for example, frowning or scrunching up your forehead or nose, it shows discomfort, confusion, or in some instances, deep concentration. None of these nonverbal cues are very attractive because no woman wants to interrupt a man who seems engrossed in deep concentration or a man who seems uncomfortable or confused.
Body turned in: To attract women and other people, always turn your body toward the person(s) you want to attract. This inviting nonverbal cue tells others that you are open to new connections, comfortable with who you are, and purposeful about meeting new people—when you are purposeful in one area of your life, you are also likely to be in other areas of	**Body turned away:** In interpersonal interactions, we turn our bodies away when we feel bored and uninterested. Likewise, failing to turn your body toward the woman or people you want to attract shows discomfort. From a broader sense, it can also show discomfort and a lack of confidence, because turning your body away is a defensive

your life, something women consider attractive.	nonverbal cue.
Stand tall: In this case, standing tall means more than how you stand. Although actually *standing* tall communicates confidence, personal power and success, it also means sitting up straighter, which shows you are comfortable with who you are, confident, open to new interactions, and ready to handle whatever life or the environment you are in throws at you. Either way, standing tall is a sign that you like who you are, something women find attractive.	**Fidgeting:** Fidgeting is a sign of discomfort and anxiety. It tells new people and women that you are not comfortable with the space you are in or confident in your ability to handle whatever comes your way.
Arms hang comfortably: What you do with your hands communicates a lot. To display personal comfort and confidence, let your hands hang comfortably by your side—if you are standing—or lay them comfortably in your lap to show openness to new interactions and deep self-confidence.	**Face touching:** When you incessantly touch your face, it communicates dishonesty and because touching your face is a manifestation of fidgeting, it shows that you are uncomfortable and nervous.
Feet planted and wide apart: When you are feeling confident and self-assured, you plant your feet firmly on the ground	**Busy feet:** Busy feet are a sign that you lack confidence and are nervous or in a stressful situation, which is why you are shuffling

because you feel capable. Planted feet placed wide apart also show that you are comfortable in the space you are in and ready for new connections, something that is very attractive.	around.
Mirroring: If you would like to attract a woman who has already seen your open body language and now seems interested, mirroring her body language will attract her to you even more. Mirroring is a sign of deep interest in someone. For instance, if the woman you want to attract is sitting in a certain way, mirroring this will make you more relatable and therefore attractive. Subtle mirroring is also a great way to appear open to new interactions, and to build rapport.	**Darting gaze:** When your gaze darts around the room or you constantly look around the room instead of at the woman you would like to attract, it says you are not interested in her, which is why you are scouting the location for another interesting or more attractive woman. It also says that you are shy and lacking confidence.
Affirmative movements: These include smiling, nodding, and a relaxed face. Movements that are positive affirm that you are empathetic, which in itself shows emotional awareness and intelligence, and that you are friendly, confident and open to new connections.	**Slumping:** A slumped posture is not attractive. It tells women and other people that you are tired, uncomfortable, and lacking confidence and self-assuredness in your ability to handle whatever life throws at you.

Steepled fingers: When you steeple your fingers or hands, it communicates authority, control, and a great sense of self-confidence. This nonverbal body language cue says you are in control and in command of yourself and are ready to tackle whatever comes your way head-on with confidence.	**Tapping fingers:** Tapping your fingers, perhaps against the counter or table, is a negative and unattractive nonverbal cue because it is a sign of nervous energy, discomfort, and a lack of self-confidence. It says you are impatient and patience is one of the character traits women find incredibly attractive.

Now that you have seen examples of strong and not-so-strong body language and nonverbal cues, use this list to discover the kind of body language you normally display.

If you discover your body language is predominantly characterized by the traits mentioned on the right-hand column of the table, you need to change this by working on your inner self-confidence and then couple that with alpha male body language.

You can do that by adopting the body language hacks on the left-hand column of the table above, so that in addition to feeling internally self-assured and confident, you also attract women by showing them that you are comfortable with who you are.

Most of all, adopting the nonverbal communication cues listed under "Positive Body Language" on the left-hand column will show women that you are friendly and open to new interactions, which will make them want to be in your presence.

In addition to keeping in mind the positive and negative body language and nonverbal cues we have discussed, also use the following strategies to increase your level of attractiveness.

Practical Alpha Male Body Language Hacks to Help You Attract Her Before You Speak a Word

NOTE: It is important that we reiterate something we mentioned earlier, which is that confident body language and alpha male nonverbal communication is physical as well as mental.

This means that even as you work on adopting the various alpha male body language hacks we shall discuss here so that you become immensely attractive to women, you should not stop working on yourself: always be working toward being a better man than you were yesterday.

That way, your confidence will continue growing deeper roots into your psyche and subconscious mind, which will ensure that displaying the following attractive and confident alpha male body language cues is easier and intuitive, something you practice because confidence and self-assuredness is what you genuinely feel within.

Cultivate a unique style.

Your style says a lot about you, and you should therefore pay special attention to it. While you are free to adopt a style that suits you best, make sure your clothes are clean, fitting, and reasonably stylish. Make sure your hair style/cut accentuates your face and look, and if you choose to accessorize, the keywords to keep in mind are: simple and stylish.

Adopt an alpha male posture.

To attract new people and women toward you, your posture needs to be strong, masculine, confident, and above all, friendly, open, and inviting; it needs to say, "I am a strong and confident man who is sure of what he wants and is open and welcoming to receiving it and new people."

You can adopt an attractive alpha male posture by doing a number of things:

- First, you need to stand like an alpha male. The general guideline here is to stand up tall and in a way that shows you have fully accepted your masculine power and are comfortable with using it. An attractive, alpha male posture involves standing with your feet comfortably apart, preferably a bit farther than shoulder width, your head held straight and high, and neck and back straight.

- As mentioned—**check table**—your hands are an important part of body language and what you do with them communicates a lot. Do not fidget, cross your arms across your chest, or use your hands to adopt any nonverbal cue that shows nervousness, lack of confidence, or anxiety. Instead, rest your arms comfortably by your side, in your lap, or in any other power pose such as steepling. If you like putting your hands in your pockets, stick out the thumbs so that you appear confident and boyishly cocky, which is attractive.

- Avoid hunching over or adopting a rigid body posture by remembering that the intention is to relax. Always hold you head and eyes high to show that you are comfortable and aware of the space you are in.

The general guideline behind adopting an attractive alpha male posture is to adopt a spread-out posture that shows you are comfortable and that tells women and new people that you are feeling good about yourself, relaxed, and open to new interactions.

More importantly, keep in mind that an alpha male posture is a result of a deeply seated sense of inner confidence and lots of practice. The best way to get better at both is to practice as often as possible by using the actionable self-confidence building habits and strategies discussed earlier, and by being conscious of your posture at any given time so that you can adapt it into a positive one.

Mind your walk.

We do it all the time and yet, how we walk is the last thing many men pay attention to; partly because most men do not realize that how we walk communicates a lot about our motivations, purpose, and inner conviction.

Whether you are walking into a room, a bar, an office, or walking toward a group of new people you would like to meet, or approaching a woman you find interesting and would like to date, you need to adopt a walk that shows purposefulness.

An alpha male walk is a walk that shows you are confident and in control of yourself. It consists of walking in an unafraid way by taking balanced and measured steps that show you know where you are going, why you are going there, and what you intend to do once you get to where you are going.

Like posture, you can change your walk in a number of ways to make it more confident and attractive.

For instance, you can:

• Make sure your steps are not too big or too small; big steps may be a sign of nervous energy or a man who is out of control, while small steps may show anxiety, meekness, or a man who is afraid. Instead, aim to take purposeful, shoulder-width apart, bold steps that communicate, "I know where I am going and why I am going there."

• Control and balance your steps by becoming consciously aware of how you walk. The more you practice conscious awareness, the easier it will be to reorient your walk, and over time confident strides will become innate to your psyche.

• To display friendliness to women and openness to meeting new people, couple a confident walk with open facial expressions, such as a smile and relaxed features, and open body language.

• Use your torso to lean into a confident walk. Do this by visualizing yourself as a man who has a buoyant spirit because he has the world rooting for him or because he is about to sign a done-deal that will change his financial fortunes or life—you can even imagine that you just achieved a massive goal or won the lottery. Move your body in a confident manner. For instance, you can walk with a slight bounce to your step to show you feel good about yourself, something women and other people find immensely attractive.

• Avoid walking too hurriedly. Remember that being an alpha male is about being in control of yourself and of your life and having a deep-seated knowledge that you can handle anything that comes your way. A hurried walk does not communicate such a message. As mentioned, adopt a swaggering gait that communicates your healthy sense of self-esteem and self-confidence.

The more you pay attention to your walk and keep in mind the alpha male walking strategies we have outlined above, the easier it will be to adjust your walk on the fly until walking like a true alpha becomes your default.

Sit like an attractive alpha.

Sitting is part of posture. When you feel insecure and unsure of yourself, you normally sit in a hunched-over posture, shoulders curled in, and chest, neck and head lowered. You are also likely to fidget with your phone or hands, or have restless feet.

Such body language and nonverbal cues are not attractive, because as mentioned earlier, they are a sign of nervous energy, fear, and a man who is very uncomfortable with himself and the space he is in; alpha males do not sit like that. They adopt confident sitting postures.

To adopt a confident posture while in a seated position, remember to relax and take as much space as you need; this shows you are comfortable and confident, a man who is sure of where he is and why he is there. If the setting and seating allows it, lean back comfortably and where possible, drape your hand over the headrest of the chair in which you are sitting.

Additionally, instead of drooping over, keep your back comfortably straight and your core and chest open; this makes you inviting and friendly, which attracts people toward you.

While in a sitting position, avoid crossing your arms in front of your chest or maintaining them in any posture that closes off your torso, which is a defensive move. When it comes to your feet, the best thing to do is to cross them at the ankle. If you are in a very comfortable situation, you can place the shin of one foot atop the thigh of the other and steeple your hands in order to come off as authoritative and in control of your space.

Use your eyes to attract and invite.

"Your eyes are the number one nonverbal cue that tells people you're an alpha male. A dominant man is not afraid to gaze directly at people. By averting your gaze, you communicate submissiveness. When you look down, you communicate self-consciousness, shame, and a sense of low status."

–John Alexander

Our eyes communicate tons of messages, which is why to attract women long before you say a word or make your first move, you need to adopt confident "eye language."

First, note that avoiding eye contact with people and with women in particular is a sign of a lack of confidence and that it tells others that you are insecure, anxious, disengaged, or being deceptive.

More importantly, failing to maintain eye contact with a woman you would like to attract is counterproductive, because by failing to maintain friendly and open eye contact how else will she be able to determine your interest?

When it comes to displaying positive eye contact, keep the following in mind:

- Avoid looking down—especially when you are walking or entering into any room. Averting your gaze downwards is against the principle of holding your head and neck high, which are positive body language cues that show confidence. Instead, keep your eyes always facing in front of you or placed on the person you would like to attract or are conversing with, in order to show interest.

- When entering a room, ensure your posture is open and confident and that your eyes are not darting everywhere. Yes, it is okay to look at things that capture your attention but it is just as important to ensure that your gaze is deliberate, which you can do by ensuring that when something or someone, perhaps a woman, captures your attention, you take a moment to observe with awareness and open curiosity. By holding eye contact for around three seconds and coupling it with an open smile and confident body language, you can attract women and new people effortlessly.

- Remember not to overdo eye contact by keeping in mind the differences between outright staring and confident eye contact. To make sure you are striking a healthy balance, hold someone's gaze to a count of three seconds, look at the person's mouth or the area below the nose for three seconds, then the eyes again, and then something else for three seconds, and continue doing this: especially when you are in a conversation with someone. This will show your interest in the person and make you more aware and engaged with the person, which is very attractive. Direct eye contact held for too long will make you come off as domineering and confrontational. The rule of thumb here is to use your intuition. Where you feel uncomfortable about maintaining eye contact for too long, maintain eye contact 50-70% of the time. In the remaining 30-50% of the time when you are not maintaining direct eye contact, use the environment—perhaps by looking to the side or at something else for a few seconds—before returning your eye contact to the person. Just make sure that in the few seconds you break eye contact, you do not look down, as it will make you appear secretive, anxious, unsure, and afraid; none of which will make you very attractive.

• Another rule of thumb is to avoid over-blinking; it shows anxiety and a low level of confidence. Control your blinking so that you feel more in control and relaxed.

The most important thing to remember about the eyes is that they communicate a lot and that you therefore need to be mindful of where you look, the length of your gaze, and the way you use them.

The best way to maintain confident and attractive eye contact is to feel good about yourself, comfortable where you are, and confident from within—so that it shows in how you conduct yourself.

Like your body, keep your eyes relaxed and inviting so that should woman you want to attract (or the people you want to meet) look your way, you can flash a seductive and inviting smile. Smiling should come easily—especially if you feel good about yourself.

In addition, remember that worry often shows in your eyes, which is why to maintain inviting and attractive eye contact, you need to work on your worries, insecurities, and fears.

The alpha handshake and confident physical touch.

If you have adopted all the above alpha male nonverbal cues and your body language shows it, you will invite and attract women. Once you do, you will eventually get a chance to date and meet people in person, which means you will need to shake hands or engage in other physical contact, such as hugs or perhaps more if the woman you are meeting is familiar and okay with respectful contact.

With handshakes, the thing to keep in mind is that above having a firm grip, you should also avoid going overboard with the handshake, perhaps by squeezing too tightly or shaking too vigorously.

Imagine the kind of handshake a confident, self-assured, and successful man would give and aim to give such a handshake. Avoid giving a dead fish handshake that makes you feel meek and afraid, and instead give a handshake that communicates that you feel in control of yourself and capable of handling the situation you are in.

Additionally, if you are meeting new people, a handshake is not just a handshake. It speaks of the person you are. For instance, if you shake someone's hand while at the same time looking around you, instead of maintaining eye contact with the person you are meeting and greeting, it will communicate a rude demeanor and disinterest, which will turn the person off.

On the other hand, if you are eager and excited to meet someone, it will show in your handshake as well as in your eye contact, posture, and mannerisms toward the person.

If you are unsure of how to give a confident handshake, here are some simple guidelines:

- When meeting new people, maintain eye contact as you approach and wear your most confident smile; when meeting women for dates, it especially pays to wear a boyish, playful, and interested smile as you approach for a handshake or to make your move.

- While maintaining eye contact and smiling as you get closer, when you are near enough, extend your arm out at the elbow to show your intention to greet the person. The person on the other end of the interaction is likely to extend his or her arm toward you.

• Once the person proffers his or her hand, offer a confident, firm handshake by connecting the web of your hand to that of the other person, curling your fingers around the person's palm, and then squeezing confidently as you pump the person's hand—no more than three times. As you do this, keep in mind that such a handshake does not mean you should crush the person's hand or shake it as if you are doing a "shake well before use" move.

With a handshake, the most important thing to keep in mind is that you want to maintain appropriate eye contact and smile before going in for the handshake, and then offer a firm, confident, and brief handshake.

" Safe" physical touches.

When it is necessary to touch women because you want to enhance the communication, to show romantic interest, or to build sexual tension, do it with confidence, because if you are at all nervous or afraid of embarrassment or rejection, the physical touch will come off the same. When you touch women confidently, it communicates a deep-seated confidence and a man who is not afraid to communicate what he likes or to pursue it; something most women consider immensely attractive.

Remember that touching is natural and that because there is nothing wrong with it, you can use it naturally in your interactions with women. The only thing you need to keep in mind here is the kind of relationship existing between you two.

If you do not have an existing relationship with a woman, it is best to stick to safe physical touches to the least sensitive parts of the body: shoulders, back, the forearm when leading her to a table for instance, or the knee if she is sitting with her knees facing toward you, which shows genuine interest.

For instance, after shaking her hand warmly and confidently, you can touch her elbow as you lead her to the table. Once you start a conversation and engage with her, depending on what you are talking about, you can smile into her eyes and briefly touch her shoulders or arms. As long as you keep in mind that the touch should be naturally flowing, confident, gentle, and playful, you have no cause for worry because your touch will enhance the connection and help you build romantic interest and sexual chemistry. If the woman's body language shows she is uncomfortable, however, then follow her cues and cease physical touching of this kind.

All the alpha male body language hacks we have covered in this chapter of the guide work: but they work only when your confidence is more than skin deep. As you practice and master these alpha male body language hacks and use them to attract women before you say a word, continue working on yourself and your insecurities, beliefs, and anything else that could be keeping you from feeling confident from within.

The next chapter talks deeply about how to continue this work to become a better man.

Chapter 4: Do the Hard Work First

Doing the hard work means committing to constant improvement as a man. Only by working toward self-betterment can you innately become a confident alpha male.

The hard work you have to put in first will largely depend on your perceived shortcomings. While these shortcomings vary from one person to the next, the aim of this chapter is to help you identify and face what is holding you back from having a great dating life.

Use the following strategies to do the hard work first, so that as you continue developing and attracting new people and women, you do so out of a desire to connect, instead of a desire to use people or to mask your insecurities.

Let us start with insecurities:

Own Your Insecurities

Insecurities are the number one killer of confidence and self-esteem, and unfortunately, it is impossible to be completely free of them because imperfections—perceived or otherwise—are part of what it means to be human.

In an earlier chapter, we talked about how confidence is about owning up to and accepting your vulnerabilities and shortcomings; even as you work toward overcoming them.

Because we live in a society inclined toward teaching men not to be vulnerable and to hide their "feelings and emotions" and therefore their insecurities, no one would blame you for thinking that being vulnerable and having insecurities will ruin your chances of dating interesting, beautiful women—or that it means you are inadequate as a man.

The fact is that hiding your insecurities is not healthy, because if you hide them you will be hiding from your authentic self. Moreover, when you hide your insecurities then instead of embracing and working on them, the insecurities steep and become negative self-talk and self-doubt that eventually manifests as an unconfident demeanor and body language that makes you unattractive to new people.

On the other hand, when you embrace your insecurities, you embrace your authentic self, and because doing so makes you aware of your perceived or real shortcomings, it becomes easier to develop a spirit of self-improvement.

As you now know, being an alpha male is about self-development, because it is about competing with who you were yesterday; something that can only come from knowing about which areas of your personality and life need improving.

Different types of insecurities.

Male insecurities come in all shapes and forms.

For instance, according to Hanalei Vierra, Ph.D. a family and marriage therapist, the most common dating insecurities in men include:

- Feeling "less than" or inadequate.
- Feeling not strong, smart, sexy, or good-looking enough.

- Feeling incapable or inexperienced with women and dating.

Melanie Greenberg, Ph.D. adds that other insecurities in men—and in most people—include:

- Fear or rejection-based insecurities.

- Insecurities based on a lack of social confidence (social anxiety).

- Insecurities based on the need to be perfect all the time.

It is best not to hide your insecurities. You need to use that energy to work on them so that you become a better man who feels confident from within, even though you have your fair share of insecurities and shortcomings.

How to embrace your insecurities: practical strategies.

To embrace, deal with, and gradually overcome your insecurities so that you enhance your chances of dating and relationship success, use the following practical strategies:

1. Start with identifying insecurities.

According to clinical psychologist Ellen Hendriksen, Ph.D., most insecurities are a result of "thinking or feeling inadequate or weirdly different."

When you think thoughts such as: "I am incompetent, ugly, awkward, boring ... I am not good-looking enough, not confident with women ..." it develops into a desire to hide these insecurities and perceived flaws.

The best way to start owning, dealing with, and then overcoming your insecurities is to start by identifying how you perceive yourself in different areas of your life.

Think deeply about what you dislike about yourself, the parts of your life and personality you do not feel good about, why you feel this way, and why you think hiding your insecurities will help you attract women.

When you do this with keen awareness and interest, you will quickly realize that most of your insecurities are only "insecurities" because you perceive them as such and because you have told yourself a negative story about them. This awareness will open you up to the possibility of adopting a new mindset toward these perceived insecurities and weaknesses, by changing the story you tell yourself about them.

This brings us to the next strategy:

2. Change your perception by minding and changing your self-talk.

Once you become more aware of your insecurities and consider why you think of these as shortcomings, commit to changing your perspective toward these different areas of your life and personality. Where your self-talk is negative and not conducive to continual self-development, change it to positive self-talk using affirmations and visualization.

If your perceived insecurity is that you are "not good-looking enough," this insecurity is nothing more than how you perceive yourself and the story you tell yourself about your outer appearance.

As such, to embrace, deal with, and then overcome such a perceived insecurity, you need to change the story you tell yourself about it. In this example, you can change the story to: "I am handsome and enough." Then you can reinforce this story by outlining and focusing on your endearing physical features and qualities.

You can even visualize yourself standing next to a drop-dead gorgeous woman who finds you enough. Doing this will change the story you tell yourself from one of insecurity to one of high self-esteem.

3. Embrace being you.

"A healthy dose of self-doubt spurs us to monitor ourselves and our interactions, and helps us identify how to get along better with our fellow humans."

—Ellen Hendriksen, Ph.D.

There is nothing wrong with having insecurities or shortcomings. Even as you go out of your way to become aware of your insecurities and to work on them, you need to understand that it is okay to have flaws and not to be perfect. In fact, embracing who you are—what we called embracing your "authentic self"—is one of the secrets to adopting an alpha male mentality and overcoming your insecurities.

Always remember that hiding your insecurities keeps you from being your authentic self. When you are not comfortable with who you are, the result is that you will always be working toward being what women want you to be, instead of who you really are or the man you know you want to become.

Moreover, embracing your authentic self is something most women find very attractive, because it shows you are confident enough to be okay with being imperfect. This gives the women you want to court and date the impetus to be comfortable with you because they understand that since you know you are not perfect, you are not looking for perfection from your dates.

4. Adopt an abundance mindset.

If specific perceived insecurities are keeping you from experiencing a thriving dating and relationship life, adopt an abundance mindset.

Here is what that means and what to do:

Dating is a numbers game. Chances are high that even if you suck at approaching women, if you continue doing it despite your awkwardness, you will eventually meet a woman who finds your awkwardness charming. Moreover, no matter how awkward or bad you are at it at first, the more you continue putting yourself out there by approaching women, the better you will get at it and the higher your chances of meeting your ideal mate.

The best way to adopt a mindset of abundance is to believe that no matter how insecure and awkward you are with women, there is someone for you out there; you just have to keep trying to find her.

Adopting this mindset is very essential because above helping you embrace your insecurities and authentic self, it does one other important thing: it helps you overcome the fear of failure and rejection and take action by talking to and approaching women.

Deal with the Fear of Dating Failure and Rejection

In the subsection about why confidence is the secret to dating success, we mentioned how the fear of failure or rejection is the primary thing that keeps you from approaching a woman you would like to date or form any sort of relationship with; we also discussed how confidence helps you overcome this challenge.

Since you already know how confidence helps you overcome fear of failure and rejection, what this subsection will do is offer you practical strategies you can use to overcome fear in the moment, so that you can take action and approach the women of your dreams:

- **Be emotionally accepting.** Let go of the belief that confident men or alpha males should not feel certain emotions that are considered "feminine," such as fear, self-doubt, sadness, anxiety, et cetera. Instead, be emotionally accepting toward every emotion you feel or experience, so that you can embrace discomfort and develop emotional resiliency. Being accepting toward your emotions will awaken you to the realization that it is normal to feel fearful when approaching women because of the chance of failure or rejection. Even confident men feel scared of rejection at times. This will help you to accept these emotions and instead of hiding them, seek ways to deal with them positively.

• **Accept the reality of rejection.** No matter how amazing, handsome, rich, successful, or confident you are, women will reject you not because you are not enough or undeserving of these women, but because rejection is integral to the dating process. Accept that out of every ten women you approach, seven or eight will reject you. If you accept this fact for what it is, you will stop seeing rejection and dating failure as proof of your unworthiness and shall instead start seeing it as a lesson-laden process that leads to the woman of your dreams. Accepting that rejection and dating failure will happen no matter what you do also allows you to realize that rejection or failure is not the end of the world, and that since it will not kill you, you can use it to become stronger and enhance your "game."

• **Never take it personally.** Rejection is never about you as a person; it is usually about your approach—or in some instances, what the woman in question is looking for in a mate. Never take rejection or dating failure personally. Instead, consider it a lesson in the sense that every rejection should tell you that you still have some work to do to iron out your approach; always remember that women reject your "pitch" or "approach" and not you as a person. If you cultivate core confidence, you will believe you are enough and deserving of romantic happiness, and you will know how to use rejection as a stepping-stone to self-betterment in your dating life.

• **Change the meaning.** According Lisa Schmidt, a dating and relationship coach, the fear of dating failure or rejection has nothing to do with the actual rejection or failure, and everything to do with the meaning you assign to it. Instead of assigning a negative meaning to failure and rejection, change it to something positive, such as using it as an indicator that your approach needs work.

It is important to remember that successful dating comes down to numbers. If you approach enough women, chances are high that as your approach improves—we called this cultivating situational confidence—so shall your chances of finding a mate who accepts you for the person you truly are.

Overcome the " Nice Guy" and " Friend Zone" Mentalities

"Just about everything a Nice Guy does is consciously or unconsciously calculated to gain someone's approval or to avoid disapproval."

—Dr. Robert Glover

The Geek Feminism Wiki defines "nice guys" and "nice guy syndrome" as: "... men who view themselves as prototypical 'nice guys' but whose 'nice deeds' are in reality only motivated by attempts to passively please women into a relationship and/or sex." This approach toward women often comes from a passive, unhealthy desire to use these nice deeds to "please and trick'" a woman into sex, dating, or a relationship.

For this guide, we can consider a "nice guy" a man who is unforthcoming with his feelings and intentions toward a woman and who uses "being nice" or "favors of all kinds" to trick a woman into a relationship.

There is nothing wrong with being a "nice" guy or person. In fact, being nice—or most importantly, *kind*—is an endearing character trait you should aim to develop as part of your self-development plan, because it is very handy in interpersonal relationships.

What differentiates being a nice person or man from a "nice guy" is the fact that when you are the latter, you are nice to women not because you truly want to be—and expect nothing in return for being this way—but because you believe being nice will get you what you want: sex, a date, or a relationship. This is a form of manipulation and inauthenticity, something you should avoid.

If getting something in return is the motivation driving your desire to be nice to a woman, you are displaying "nice guy" tendencies. This is because being truly nice to a woman should have no strings attached to it; it should come naturally without any expectations of reciprocity.

It is very common to hear "nice guys" complain that the women they want reject them because they "only date bad boys." This is nothing but a justification made by a man who is being covert with his feelings and intention toward a woman, and who is now feeling bitter because the woman does not reciprocate his "niceness" with what he wants.

Here is the thing, adopting a "nice guy" mentality toward dating and relationships, perhaps by being emotionally available for a woman you want—expecting that she will fall into your arms—goes against everything we have talked about when it comes to being a confident, alpha male. If you do such a thing expecting the woman in question to fall into your arms, your deception will backfire because in her mind, you are just being nice without expecting anything in return, and because a "real man" expresses what he feels, does everything he can to get it, and then lets the chips fall where they may.

How to let go of the " nice guy" syndrome.

To overcome the "nice guy" mentality, use the following strategies:

• **Redefine the issue.** The distinction between being nice and being a "nice guy" is that the latter attaches ulterior motives to being nice to women and uses it as a covert way to get sex or into a relationship. There is no reason why you should stop being nice with women; in fact, being nice by treating women kindly and with respect is a hallmark trait of a true alpha male. What you should do is stop attaching ulterior motives to being nice to women because that goes against the principles of being confident enough to speak what is in your heart. Moreover, being covert about your feelings will not get you anywhere, and using niceness to get a woman into bed only proves that you are not a "nice guy" but a manipulative jerk.

- **Be confident enough to stand up for what you want.** This is the quintessential way to overcome the "nice guy" syndrome. "Nice guys" do not openly communicate their desire toward a woman because they are afraid of rejection or failure. This fear of failure or rejection is what drives them into using "being nice" and other covert methods to get into a relationship. You can avoid this by openly communicating what you want; if you get rejected, you can learn from it and use it to better your approach for the next time you put yourself out there.

- **Embrace masculinity.** One of the primary reasons why "nice guys" are so covert with their intentions toward the women they desire has to do with the fact that they do not feel deserving enough, which is why they use covert means to win women over. Such a level of dishonesty will not get you the results you want. Instead, embrace your masculinity and authentic self so that you become a man who is not afraid to express his desires or to go after what he wants.

Above all, to let go of the "nice guy" mentality of thinking that you can trick a woman into bed or a relationship by being nice to her; passively pursuing her; or being too assuming or overly pleasing and available to her, cultivate core confidence and adopt the alpha male mindset.

"She friend-zoned me," is a very common complaint among "nice guys" who did not get their way. You need to understand one thing:

The " friend zone" does not exist.

If you type: "What is the friend zone?" into Google's search bar, the first result defines the friend zone as:

"A situation where a friendship exists between two people but one of the people involved in the friendship has an unreciprocated romantic or sexual interest in the other."

Source: Oxford University Press. "Friend zone." Lexico.com

http://www.lexico.com/definition/friend_zone (accessed January, 2020).

The friend zone is a "make believe world" created by "nice guys." Out of the desire to justify their fear of rejection, they assume that the women have "friend zoned" them, because they are not reciprocating their "niceness" with love.

This "zone" does not exist, because when you meet women, one of two things can happen: friendship or a romantic relationship. First, you have the option to communicate your dating interests and intentions toward her, at which point she can reject you and you can move on to another woman. Second, you can try to maneuver your way into her pants by deceiving her that you are a "nice, friendly man" who just wants to be her friend—but deep down, you are scheming and using being nice as leverage to get into a relationship with her. If you choose the latter option, you have no one to blame if the woman you want "friend-zones" you.

You have complete control over the relationship that forms between you and women—and all people for that matter. If you want to date a woman, communicate it openly by asking her out on a date. If she rejects you, decide if you would like to move on or to continue having her in your life as a platonic friend: not because you eventually intend to turn her into a romantic partner, but because you want to be genuine friends with her.

The situation called the "friend zone" is a result of miscommunicated intentions or desires. It therefore does not exist because being friends with a woman and hoping that this will implicitly communicate what you feel and lead to sex or dating is deceptive, and as such, not the best foundation for a relationship of any kind.

The only way to get out of the proverbial "friend zone" is to avoid getting into it in the first place, by openly and confidently communicating your intentions toward a woman.

Figure out What You Want

A core prerequisite to success with dating interesting and beautiful women is to figure out what you want and to define it as clearly as possible.

As part of working on yourself first, it is very important that you clearly describe the kind of woman you want, the kind of relationship you want now and in the future, and the kind of standards you intend to apply to your romantic partners and relationships.

How to define what you want in a match.

To find a good match, you need to have a clear idea of what you want in a woman and in a relationship.

Use the following tips to define this:

- **Consider your core values.** According to Lori Bizzoco, a public relations expert and relationship coach, thinking about your core values is the best way to figure out what you want in a partner and in your dating and relationship life. This is because when your core values are the guides you use to determine whether you should or should not date a woman, it becomes easier to get into healthy, mutually satisfying relationships.

- **Reorient your expectations.** While there is nothing wrong with having expectations about dating, love, and relationships, you need to reconsider any predetermined or unrealistic expectations you may have toward how your partner should look, behave, and how the relationship should pan out, et cetera. Consider how your upbringing, experiences, and beliefs influence the kind of partner and relationship you want, and where those expectations are not healthy, realistic—or even important—reorient or change them altogether.

- **Define what is important.** In their article "Dating Tips for Finding the Right Person," authors Jeanne Segal, Ph.D., Lawrence Robinson, and Greg Boose, from HelpGuide.org, note that the best way to figure out what you want in your dating and relationship life is to figure out what you consider important and want/need in a partner. When it comes to "wants," the authors note that you should define physical attributes such as hair color, weight and height, intellect, occupation, et cetera. Most of your "wants" are negotiable and adaptable. When it comes to "needs"— the kind of partner you need—they note that these non-negotiables include core values, goals, and ambitions. By defining both, it becomes easier to create a benchmark standard that you can use to determine if a potential partner suits you. (http://helpguide.org/articles/relationships-communication/tips-for-finding-lasting-love.htm accessed January, 2020.)

Looking beyond the strategies above, the best way to figure out what you want in a partner or in a relationship is to embrace your authentic self and use this knowledge to determine the kind of partner or relationship you want and need, based on your purpose and ultimate aims in life.

If you would like some more help with the considerations you should have in mind as you figure out what you want, use the resource page below:

http://bit.ly/2r8yE2k

Take everything you have learned from the various chapters within this section, use it to better yourself and become a confident man, and then couple it with the various strategies discussed.

The next section will be highly practical in the sense that it will show you how to use what you have learned in this section to unlock the secrets to meeting people in real-life; when using online dating apps; and how to attract women on dates.

Section 3:

The Quintessential Dating Guide for the Modern Man – How to Navigate the Dating Scene like a Pro

The various chapters that make up this section of the guide offer practical, hands-on advice you can use to confidently navigate the modern dating scene.

Among other things, we shall discuss:

- Offline dating strategies you can use to meet women and new people in real-life; more importantly, how to approach these women confidently and in a self-assured manner that gets results.

- How to use online dating apps and platforms correctly and avoid common online dating mistakes.

We shall also discuss a ton of other topics and strategies that when combined with everything you learned in the first two sections of the guide, should help you to navigate the modern dating scene like a pro.

Chapter 5: Where to Meet Women (and People) In "Real" Life

Despite the popularity of online dating and the proliferation of online dating apps and platforms, meeting people offline, (what we are calling meeting people in "real-life,") is one of the best ways to meet women and new people and to create amazing connections and relationships.

As a matter of fact, research conducted by FullScreen.com, an agency that tracks trends, showed that out of every ten people aged 18-34, 61% dislike online dating so much that given the choice between staying single and using online dating, they would rather stay single.

The study also noted that because of the impersonal nature of online dating—since all you have to do is swipe right or left—as much as 76% of research participants prefer organic dating or meeting someone offline.

Part of the reason why meeting people in real-life is popular has to do with the fact that unlike meeting women and new people online, meeting them offline is much more personal and involved. This is because you are interacting with an actual person, which makes it easier to gauge interest by reading body language as well as nonverbal cues, and to form genuine connections.

Meeting people and women in real-life situations may be nerve-wracking, but once you get past the initial discomfort of connecting with people on a very personal basis, it beats online dating in many ways—not that there is anything wrong with online dating.

The aim of this chapter is to show you how to go about meeting new people and women offline.

Where to Meet People and Where to Find Likeminded People

Meeting new people and women offline is an amazing way to embrace discomfort, callous your mind, develop emotional resiliency, and become aware of your interpersonal strengths and weaknesses, all of which tie back to what it means to be a confident, alpha male.

You can meet new people and find women in a number of ways. Below are the most effective of these ways:

- **Get out as much as possible.** To meet new people and find potential matches and dates offline, you need to go out as often as possible and as much as possible. For instance, you can head out to the park, the fair, the movies, the local coffee shop, festivals, et cetera. The more you get out by giving up the temptation to become a homebody or hermit, the easier it shall be to meet like-minded people.

- **Use Meetup Apps.** Meetup apps, such as Meetup, Nextdoor, and Bumble, curate in-person "meetups" organized by like-minded people. For example, if you like cooking, programming, romantic poetry, book clubs, hiking, or sports, you can use such apps to find and attend related local events where you can find people and women who have similar interests to you.

- **Go out to town and bars.** Bars are a great way to meet women and new people thanks to the already implied social nature of the setting. When meeting women at a bar—and in real-life in general—it is very important that you become mindful of how you go about it. First, remember to be stylish because as research from Peter Jonason, Ph.D. noted, a disheveled appearance is a great turn off for women. Second, remember to display open and approachable body language because as another study conducted in 2010 concluded, it takes about three minutes to make a first impression and for a woman to conclude whether she likes you or not. Most of all, to ensure you create an actual connection, be sure of what you want and purposeful about it. For instance, if you do not want to "hook up," aim to get her number after a few minutes of a good conversation—it is always better to end a conversation on a high note-and be certain to communicate that you intend to use the phone number to plan a date elsewhere.

- **Chance meetings.** If you have always wanted a "meet cute," then places like the gym, the supermarket, the subway and other modes of public transport, et cetera, are great for random and chance meetups. The most important thing to keep in mind about chance meetings is that you have to enter them confidently. Yes—at first, talking to random women at the supermarket or gym will scare you and you will probably suck at it. However, if you keep in mind the confident man and alpha male body language strategies we discussed earlier, you should be okay, and if you keep putting yourself out there, taking chances, and being vulnerable, you will eventually meet an amazing woman.

- **At work.** Meeting women at work and work related events is another great way to find possible dating partners. With this option, in addition to displaying confident body language and being stylish, purposeful, and self-assured, so that the woman you want to attract notices you, be aware of any existing policies about dating within the work environment.

You can meet amazing women and new people in many other places, such as at parks, retreats, charities, local classes, and restaurants.

When it comes to meeting women and new people offline, the most important thing you need to do is simply go out with the intention to talk to and interact with women.

As mentioned in the first section about gaining confidence, you will probably suck at starting conversations with women, but the more you practice, the stronger your core and situational confidence shall grow and the better you will become.

Chapter 6: How to Cut through the Crap and Navigate the Online Dating Scene like a Pro

You can probably relate to trying to find love or a date online without any luck. You are not alone or to blame—well, perhaps you are to blame if you are committing the various mistakes that we will cover in this chapter.

If you have not had much luck with online dating, your lack of knowledge is at fault. See, to achieve success with online dating and start conversations with women in a way that gets them to respond, and then to lead those conversations forward until it culminates into a date offline, you need to know how to cut through the crap and navigate the online dating scene like a pro.

The aim of this chapter is to equip you with invaluable strategies you can use to do just that—so that after learning how to use online dating apps and platforms properly, you can meet women—and out of the following conversations, meetings, and dates, find an interesting woman based on what you want.

Let us start by discussing the number-one reason why many men fail to achieve success with online dating.

The #1 Reason You Are Yet to Find Success

with Online Dating

Here is the major reason why you have not yet achieved success with online dating: your online dating profile is unclear about what you want and does not help you put your best foot forward, or do a very good job of aptly describing who you are as a man.

One of the things we discussed at length in the first section of this guide is the fact that alpha males know what they want and are not afraid to communicate it openly and confidently. This applies to online dating as well.

Professor Harry Reis, Ph.D., notes that online dating profiles make it difficult to discern important relational elements, such as someone's principles, whether the person is an effective communicator, et cetera. He does, however, note that by clearly stating who you are and what you want, and by being true to this person, you can eliminate most of these difficulties.

Cutting through the "crap," by populating your online dating with all relevant information about who you are and what you want, is integral to your success with online dating. This is partly because when what you want and who you are is clear on your profile, you are that much more likely to find a compatible partner, because as a **research study published by Andrew T. Fiore and Judith S. Donath** noted, "People tend to fall for what is familiar."

Additionally, according to Lara Hallam, Ph.D., when you are honest about who you are and what you want, it becomes easier to find someone who has similar interests. Matching with familiar people makes it more probable that when you message a match, you are that much more likely to end up talking and eventually meeting for a date offline. This is because you already have a mutual interest, a level of familiarity, and a topic you can use to start a conversation.

Being honest about who you are and what you want to get out of being on an online dating app or platform, eliminates surprises and awkward moments down the line when you meet the person. For instance, being honest about your weight, age, or occupation ensures that when you finally do meet a match, she does not get the surprise of her life.

To recap, irrespective of which online dating platform or app you decide to use, ensure you are honest about what you want and who you are. In addition to helping you find compatible matches, it will also help you to optimize your profile in a manner that shows you are a man who has embraced his authentic self and knows who he is.

Now that we are talking about it, let us delve a bit deeper into how to create and optimize your online dating profile to ensure it attracts the right matches.

How to Create a Memorable, Honest, and Engaging Online Dating Profile

To create a memorable, honest and engaging online dating profile that attracts matches and leaves the right impression, first, pay attention to the principle of authenticity and honesty, as described above. When you are honest about who you are, what you want, or the kind of relationship/woman you are searching for, you are more likely to find better matches.

In addition to doing the above, the following strategies will help you to create an engaging online dating profile that stands out:

- **Consider your username and headline.** With usernames, you can use your real name; if you prefer a different username, choose one that is attention grabbing and meaningful. The general guideline here is to choose a username that expresses who you are and—where possible—lets women know something about you. For instance, if you are a mechanic called John, a username such as "FixitJohn" works because it is playful and linked to what you do. When it comes to your headline, keep in mind that its intention is to grab attention and leave women wanting to know more about you. To create a standout headline, think of which few words you would use to market yourself and generate interest if you were a product.

- **Fill out your profile.** Leaving your profile blank is a big no! Take advantage of the profile-filling options available to you depending on which online dating program you are using. Data from online dating site Zoosk.com has shown that when you fill out your username, you are likely to get 20% more messages, and when you fill out your description, your chances of receiving messages and replies jumps to 28%. On the issue of what to write in your description, simply think about what you would want potential matches to know about you, what you want, and who you are. Then, use a positive, conversational tone to describe yourself well, keeping in mind the principle of authenticity. Aim to describe yourself in a way that ensures what makes you different shines through.

- **Avoid overdoing it.** Although you should go out of your way to fill out your profile, according to Sameer Chaudhry from the University of North Texas, your profile description should not be a long essay. Chaudhry notes that your description should get to the point and include what makes you interesting, who you are, and what you are looking for. According to research, you can create the perfect online dating profile by focusing 70% of the profile on describing who you are, and 30% on what you want. In practice, create two short paragraphs describing yourself—what makes you interesting, things you like, et cetera—and one short paragraph describing what you want.

• **Mention romance in your profile.** According to data from Zoosk.com, mentioning the words "romance" or "romantic" can increase your message rate by 41%; mentioning the phrase "hopeless romantic" increases your message rate by 38%; while using the term "old-fashioned" increases your message rate 16%. As you fill out your profile description, think about how you can work such phrases into the bio—but remember to do so only if you are actually romantic or old-fashioned, after all, honesty is the best policy.

Above all else, to create a dating profile that is unique, memorable, and honest, remember to embrace your authentic self and let this personality shine through. When you are authentic, you will describe yourself in an honest and interesting way that will help you attract the kind of person you want.

In addition to the above tips, also pay attention to your photos.

How to Make Your Photo(s) Count and Stand Out

Most online dating apps and platforms have the option of uploading five-to-ten photos depending on the actual platform. While there are no rules stating you should fill up your photo slots, it is best to do so. More importantly, it is essential that you upload photos that show what you are about and that match your description. Keeping this in mind:

• Upload photos that accurately describe your present self, which means no photos of your twenties if you are well into your thirties.

• Make sure that out of the five-to-ten photo slots available, at least two are action shots that show you doing something you enjoy doing, such as kayaking, running, or even playing the guitar.

- Additionally, because the aim of photos is to capture interest in who you are as a person, restrict social photos with friends to a maximum of two.

- For your profile picture, use a photo that shows your face clearly, which means you should avoid photos where you are wearing hats or sunglasses, group photos, blurry photos, et cetera. Instead, go for shots that show you smiling at the camera, so that you appear confident, friendly, and open to meeting new people; or use a photo where you are doing something that fills you with joy but where you are still looking at the camera and smiling. According to data from Zoosk.com, a profile picture where you are smiling can increase your match and message rate by up to 46%.

- When it comes to full-frame photos, avoid topless selfies and instead use an outdoor full-body shot. Data from Zoosk.com further indicated that a full-body photo increases messages by up to a whopping 203%, while an outdoor photo increases the message rate by up to 19%.

- Mix up your photos by avoiding all selfies or photos where you are doing the same thing. As you think about which mix of photos to use, keep in mind that the idea is to use the photos to accentuate your description, to show who you are—and more importantly, to show what you are about and what makes you interesting.

After optimizing your profile using the strategies highlighted above, your match rates will improve significantly. From here, the next step is to interact with your matches by starting interesting conversations.

How to Open Conversations with Your

Online Matches

Starting conversations with matches is a nerve-wracking experience for most men; it does not have to be if you know what you are doing.

Apply the following strategies to make the process easier and to open conversations that get results; in a way that shows you are respectful, "safe to date," and someone she should know:

• **Do a bit of reconnaissance first.** Researching your potential date a little bit is not creepy; it is doing your due diligence. Once you match with a woman you fancy, before you say "hi," which is what 90% of men do, take a moment to look over her profile and pictures. Notice anything that stands out about her profile and pictures so that you can use it as inspiration for part of your opening message. Do not overthink it though; you can start a conversation on just about anything, such as her passions, mutual interests, some of her pictures, et cetera.

• **Ace the opener.** The opening message is usually the most frightening for men, which is somewhat understandable because how you open the conversation will largely determine the direction of the interaction. The best way to start a conversation with an online match is to start by referencing something in her profile. Yes, you can open with a funny, seductive, nerdy, or sweet opener that feels authentic to your personality, but the openers that get the responses are usually those that reference the woman's profile. This is because when you mention something about your potential date's profile, the fact that you took the time to read it carefully and notice some elements lets her know that you are genuinely interested in her.

• **Avoid superficial clichés.** Even if she is your most beautiful match yet, avoid mentioning beauty in your initial interaction or using words such as beautiful, gorgeous, stunning, et cetera. Your potential date receives superficial messages from men all day. One of the things researchers Sameer Chaudhry and Khalid Khan noted in their study about converting online contact into a first date, is that "we routinely reject unrealistically positive views of ourselves, because this raises suspicion about the motives of the complimenter." (https://ebm.bmj.com/content/20/2/48, accessed January, 2020.) When you use such words in your initial conversation, your potential date will quickly distrust you. Instead, tailor your message by referencing something in her profile.

• **Keep things light and a bit flirty.** If she responds to your opening message, respond with a light, positive, and somewhat flirty message keeping in mind that the aim is to move the conversation along to an actual date. You cannot go wrong with genuine answers and replies that bring a smile to her face. It will show her you are interesting and create the desire to want to know you more. Keep the conversation flirty by avoiding "heavy" or "difficult" conversations.

• **Follow up.** If you are truly interested in a woman who does not respond to your first message, do not assume she is not interested, especially if you thought-out your message; she may be busy. Instead, after two days of no response, write her a lighthearted follow-up message but refrain from sending more than one follow-up message, which will be frustrating and a big turn off.

• **Keep the conversation going.** Once you are chatting with a woman, there is an easy way to keep the conversation going and building up toward a date: if you have asked a question and she replies, respond to it, then give your answer to the same question, and then ask her something else related. Every conversation you have with a woman is a chance to show her the positive traits that make you an amazing man to date and in the case of online dating, to progress the conversation toward a date.

Becoming great at starting conversations with online matches is a matter of practice and having fun with it; while you will not be successful all the time, which is okay, as long as you remember to have fun with it, and are genuinely interested in your matches and patient with the process, you should come out ahead.

With online dating but with messaging especially, you need to be very mindful of committing silly mistakes that turn women off.

Dos and Don' ts of Online Dating (Especially Messaging)

When using online dating platforms and apps, and when messaging your matches, keep the following in mind:

Do:

- Start your messages with a greeting.

- Be flirty and spontaneous.

- Ask your potential date questions that pique her interest and get her to respond intelligently; this is how you will know which women to ask out.

- Be genuinely interested in getting to know her; it will show in the messages you send and the questions you ask.

- Have an open mind and be honest and authentic.

- Be prepared for failure and to get no response from women because like offline dating, online dating and messaging is a numbers game; the more you message women with genuine interest, the better you will get at it and the higher your chances of success.

- Have boundaries and rules about conversation topics and meetups.

- Be patient and keep trying.

Don' t:

- Don't overshare too much personal information on your profile or before meeting a woman in person; being safe with your information pays off.

- Don't text her large paragraphs; instead, mirror her response and only text her longer messages when she does so to, and move the conversation toward a date because the fact that she is texting you longer messages shows her interest.

- Don't send copy-pasted messages or replies; women can sense such things.

- Avoid overusing emojis; in fact, keep your emoji usage to no more than two per message.

- Don't be antagonizing; instead, be flirty and playful by remembering that the intention of online conversations is to build interest and to make her feel comfortable so that when you ask her out, she says yes.

- Don't send unsolicited photos—especially those of an explicit nature; women hate that and do not respond well to it.

- Don't talk about your ex or even mention the last date you were on.

- Don't be too expectant. Remember that unlike offline dating, women need to get a bit comfortable with you—a stranger they've never met—before they say yes to you.

- Don't be too forward; ease a woman into a date by showing interest in her and build rapport; that way, she is more likely to say yes when you do ask her out.

• Avoid pretending to be someone you are not because other than being a deceptive maneuver, it will only breed failure and disappointment.

• Don't let yourself become a pen pal; move the conversation toward an actual date.

The aim of online conversations with women is to lead the conversation toward a date. You can do that in a number of ways:

How to Move the Conversation into a Real-Life Date

To drive a conversation with a match toward an offline date, implement the following strategies:

- **Make her feel comfortable.** The rule of connectivity notes that when we feel connected to someone, the person becomes more attractive and persuasive. You can use this to your advantage by mirroring a woman's response and communication style. If she opens her messages a certain way, copy it; if she sends messages of a certain length, mirror it. If she is using emojis, use them too but avoid overdoing it. The more you mirror her, the more familiar you shall be and the easier it shall be for her to say yes when you eventually ask her out.

- **Use every interaction as an opportunity.** Every conversation you have with an online match is an opportunity to drive the conversation toward a date. If you are talking about interests and she asks what you do on weekends, tell her about how you intend to spend your Saturday. For example: you will be taking your niece to watch the new Frozen Movie in the morning, your dog for a walk in the park in the afternoon, and then meet some friends in the evening for something interesting. Ask her if she would like to join the evening soiree. The fact that it is a group event is likely to appeal to her significantly.

- **Do not take too long.** Remember that your match is not on an online dating platform or app to find a pen pal; she wants to date and you should therefore not take too long before suggesting an offline date. In fact, research data analyzed by dating experts from VIDA Select showed that the best time to ask a woman out on a date is after two or three replies.

• **Notice the signs.** If the two-to-three replies tip above does not cut it for you, pay attention to how your match responds to your messages. If she sends you longer-than-conventional messages, casually ask her to meet up because you like talking to her and would enjoy hearing her responses in person. If she uses emojis or "LOL" in her messages to you, she is telling you to ask her out because you are interesting enough to make her laugh. Make a move and ask her out by suggesting you meet up at a place you would both enjoy (reconnaissance will come in very handy here). If she asks you questions, she is curious, which means she would probably say yes if you asked to meet up for some food, music, a hike, or whatever else you may have in mind that you think she would enjoy doing with you.

• **Suggest a meet up instead of a date:** Meeting new people can be scary. Instead of explicitly asking her out for a date— "let's go out on a date"—ask her out by suggesting a meetup. This keeps things casual. The caveat to this is to become attentive of the kind of woman she is. If she seems like someone who would respond better to "date" instead of "meetup," go with your gut.

• **Make plans.** Once she says yes to the meetup, take control, and set a definite plan; confident men are not afraid to make plans. You can give her limited options such as jazz and drinks on Friday evening, or a fun Saturday afternoon event. Keep this message short and at the tail end of it, message her your phone number and ask her to send hers so that you can coordinate in case of last-minute changes to the plan.

Above all this, remember that confident men know what they want and are not afraid of communicating it openly. Be confident when asking her out and make a definite plan.

For instance, tell her about a pub you heard about that serves amazing seafood and plays great jazz—if she likes seafood and jazz—and comfortably suggest that you check it out together. If you both like concerts, tell her about a concert you really want to attend and ask if she would like to go with you.

Like starting conversations with women offline, driving the conversation toward a date and then asking her out is a matter of practice; the more you do it, the better you will get at it—and know what works and what does not.

Now that you have a date in the books, you need to navigate the first meeting or date like a pro so that it leads to a genuine connection and another date. Here is what to do.

Five Tips on What to Do on That First Real-Life Meeting

During the first real-life meeting with your match, pay attention to the various confidence and alpha male strategies we discussed earlier and observe the following too:

> 1. **Mind your first impression.** You want your first impression to be a lasting one; while you should embrace your authentic self and do what feels comfortable, remember that the more stylish and confident you are during that initial interaction, the more intrigued she will be, and the more she will want to know you, which is what you want. Make a great first impression by dressing well, walking tall, maintaining eye contact and having open body language, shaking her hand well, and perhaps touching her hand as you guide her toward your table. The idea is to create chemistry and if you are

confident, which you should be if you have worked on everything we talked about in the first section of the guide, this will all come naturally.

2. Respect her schedule by being punctual. Remember that confident men have a purpose; as such, they value time. Show her that you respect her by being punctual. Do not be late to your date; instead, arrive a few minutes early (fifteen to thirty minutes early should do) and use that time to familiarize yourself with the location. Keeping time will impress your date immensely and tell her that you made the effort because your interest in her is genuine.

3. Mind how you start the conversation. After meeting up and exchanging "hello" and other pleasantries, be very mindful of how you lead the conversation. You want the initial conversation to be comfortable and a bit playful, so that your date starts feeling comfortable. If your online conversation left off somewhere interesting, you can carry that on, and if not, keep in mind that the initial moments are about getting comfortable with being in each other's presence in real-life, which means the conversation should be positive and about something familiar. Make sure too that as the conversation progresses, it is lighthearted and fun; first dates are difficult enough already. Talking about "heavy" stuff will only lead to further awkwardness.

4. Give her a chance to speak. The nervousness of meeting your match for the first time can cause you to blubber on like a moron. Avoid the temptation of doing all the talking or wanting to fill every silence with talk. As is the case with online conversations, ask your date interesting questions, respond to her answers, and as mentioned earlier, use every response and interaction as a chance to drive the conversation forward.

5. Be present. This is the most important tip of the list. You are on a date with this woman because you want to know her on a personal level and perhaps use that to determine if she is "the one." Be there, present and connect with her by turning off all distractions such as your phone so that you can give her your undivided attention and make her feel as if in that moment she is the center of your focus. Look into her eyes as she talks to you, display open and affirmative body language when she says something you agree with, listen to her keenly so that you can understand her well and respond intelligently, and so that you can take cues from her responses and use what she says to keep the conversation flowing.

If this is too much to take in, here is a simple trick to have in mind during your first offline meeting with your match: be authentic, genuinely interested in knowing her, and remember to be confident inside out so that you display attractive body language that draws her in. If you do this, your first date should go very well and lead to another.

Chapter 7: Types of Questions to Ask to Start a Conversation and Keep It Going

While these questions work best online, you can also use them offline to start conversations with women and new people:

" Would you rather ..." questions.

"Would you rather ..." questions such as: "Would you rather travel ten years into the past or the future?" are great because they show you are interesting and intelligent, and because they reveal a lot about a person's values and personality.

Challenge questions.

Challenge questions challenge your match to give you an interesting answer to a question. For instance, you could give your match a varied list of ingredients in your fridge and ask her what kind of meal she would prepare you for dinner. If food is not your cup of tea, you can challenge her to imagine you are planning a vacation together and have X amount of money that she should use to plan an amazing adventure.

" This or that" questions.

"This or that" questions get a match to reveal her personality and likes. For instance, you can ask a match, "Book first and then movie *or* movie first and then book?"

" If ..." questions.

Questions starting with "If ..." are amazing; in addition to being great conversation starters, they lead to deep, interesting conversations. For instance, when you ask a match, "If you could be have one super ability, which ability would you pick?" then in addition to getting her to reveal her personality, she is likely to reply with something interesting that you can use to lead the conversation, such as her asking in reply about which super ability you would choose and why.

Fun fact questions.

"Did you know that thirty-three percent of online daters form a relationship?" Did that catch your interest?

Fun fact questions, what we call "Did you know ...?" questions, are a fantastic way to start a conversation in an interesting way, and when done right, they are a great way to keep the conversation going too, because they are very entertaining.

Genuine questions are a great way to start a conversation and keep it going because they show you are truly interested in your potential date—interested enough to ask her questions so that you can know her better.

When using questions to start a conversation, the most important thing you need to keep in mind is you should ask the questions in a way that compels a response.

Chapter 8: What Not to Do – Common Dating Pitfalls Most Women Really Hate

We have covered a lot thus far and without a doubt, you know what to do and what not to do to attract women and new people, start conversations, and keep them going.

This short section is a reminder of common dating mistakes most men commit online and offline that women hate, which can ruin your chances of dating and relationship success:

- **Unsolicited photos.** Under no circumstance should you send women unsolicited pictures of your penis (otherwise called "dick pics"). In fact, unless you have cultivated a conversation, avoid sending your match pictures in the initial conversations, even memes, because using pictures instead of communicating directly tells her you are not making an effort to get to know her, which tells her you are not that into her.

- **Being too forward, creepy, or sexual in initial communication.** Do not commit this common mistake. Being too forward is a costly mistake because it fails to give the woman a chance to get comfortable with you. Being sexual in the initial communication is another costly mistake you should not make, because it tells a woman that you are an internet creep looking for sexual conquests.

• **Over eagerness.** Over eagerness is very similar to being too forward, except in this case, you push and pressure her into going out on a date long before she shows signs of readiness. Over eagerness denies you a chance to build attraction and is a big turn off; instead, engage her in an interesting, rapport-building conversation so that she becomes comfortable with you.

• **Being self-centered.** Avoid being too self-centered by talking her ear off about your day, work, et cetera. Remember that at heart, whether you are chatting online or talking to a woman in person, your aim is to cultivate chemistry. The best way to do that is to ask her questions about her life, interests, hobbies, work, et cetera, and to give her a chance to talk. When you show interest in her life, she will consider you a valuable man because women love a man that listens.

• **Not being genuine and authentic.** Under no circumstance should you lie about who you are; in addition to going against the principles of authenticity and what it means to be a confident, alpha male, lying about things such as your age, circumstances, weight and body type, occupation, relationship status, kids, et cetera, will only lead to disappointment and eroded trust. Once you lose a woman's trust, getting it back is no walk in the park.

• **Seeking sympathy.** Avoid the common mistake of self-deprecating or putting yourself down in a bid to fish for compliments or sympathy; that is a "nice guy" move that is likely to backfire on you—not just because it is manipulative, but because the truth will come out eventually, and guess what? The result will be disappointment all round.

• **Grammar mistakes.** Avoid grammatical mistakes and use correct spellings. Doing otherwise will tell your match that you were in a hurry to text her and perhaps a thousand other women. Moreover, failing to use correct spelling and making grammatical mistakes is likely to lead to miscommunication, which you do not want. A confident man takes pride in what he says and how he says it; be that man!

The worst mistake you can commit is that of letting the fear of failure or rejection hold you back or keep you from making your move. Take the dive and open up a conversation; develop camaraderie with a few back and forth messages, and then ask her out.

Conclusion

Thank you for reading this guide *Dating for Men: Unlocking the Secrets to Meeting People in Real-Life and Using Online Dating Apps – Along with How to Attract Women on Dates by Displaying Alpha Male Confidence and Body Language.* It should have set you up with all the skills and insight you need to become a dating pro, capable of meeting and attracting the woman of your dreams.

As you have seen, meeting people online and in real life is relatively easy if you know what you are doing. This book has given you everything you need to cut through the crap to attract women by displaying confident body language and by adopting an alpha male mindset.

Remember that to achieve success in your dating life, you need to cultivate confidence and embrace your authentic self. If you do that, you will display attractive body language that will help you attract interesting women and new people. You will be happier within yourself and have the right attitude and approach to experience plenty of dating successes along the way.

If you enjoyed this guide to dating for the modern man, a review on Amazon is always appreciated.

Now go out there and start confidently meeting some amazing women!

Check out another book by Kory Heaton

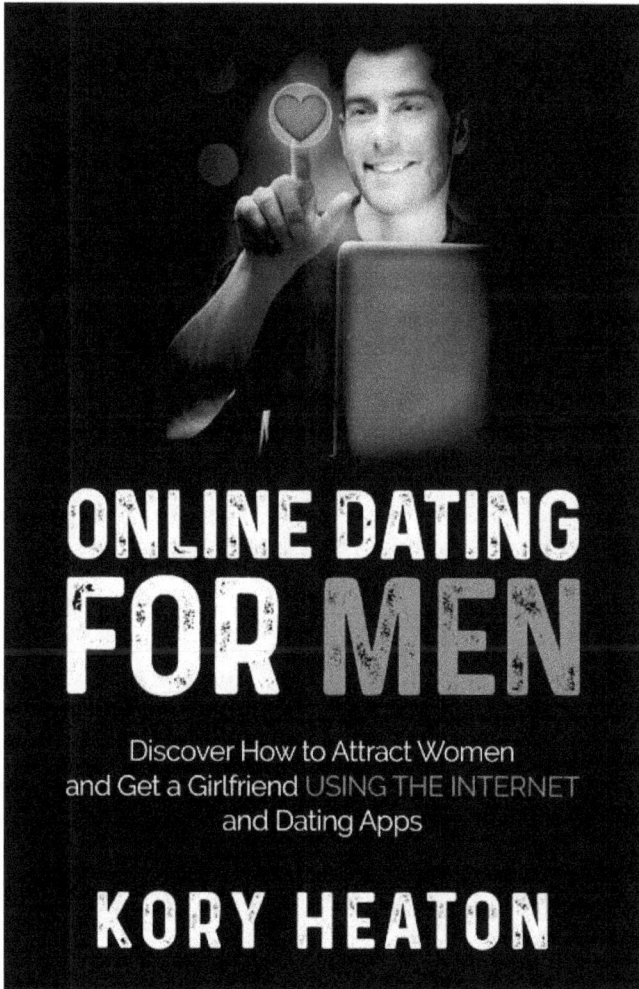

ONLINE DATING
FOR MEN

Discover How to Attract Women
and Get a Girlfriend USING THE INTERNET
and Dating Apps

KORY HEATON

www.ingramcontent.com/pod-product-compliance
Lightning Source LLC
Chambersburg PA
CBHW070800300326
41914CB00053B/754